BEAUTY FOR ASHES

BEAUTY FOR ASHES

Receiving Emotional Healing

JOYCE MEYER

WARNER Faith®

NEW YORK BOSTON NASHVILLE

Warner Books Edition

Warner Faith

Time Warner Book Group
1271 Avenue of the Americas, New York, NY 10020
Visit our Web site at www.twbookmark.com.

Printed in the United States of America

First Warner Books Edition: November 2003
10

Library of Congress Cataloging-in-Publication Data
Meyer, Joyce
Beauty for ashes : receiving emotional healing / Joyce Meyer. — Rev. ed.
p. cm.
Includes bibliographical references.
ISBN: 978-0-446-69115-4
ISBN: 0-446-69115-1
1. Adult child sexual abuse victims—Religious life. 2. Meyer, Joyce, 1943– I. Title.

BV4596.A25M48 2003
248.8'6—dc21 2003053504

I wish to dedicate this book to my husband, Dave, who showed me the love of Jesus while my healing was in progress.

Thank you, Dave, for letting me be me, even when I was not very pleasant; for always being patient and positive; and for trusting God to change me when it looked impossible.

I believe this work is yours as well as mine, and I thank God that He chose to bring you into my life. You truly have always been my "knight in shining armor."

Contents

Introduction

If your joy is hindered because of emotional pain, if you have been abused or have suffered from feelings of rejection, I encourage you to read this book. If you have ever listened to my radio or television broadcasts, you have heard me speak of the fact that I was abused throughout my childhood and teenage years. In fact, my life was like a heap of ashes before I met the Lord and was set free by the truth of His Word.

This is not a story of all the unpleasant details of my own past, but I do share enough about my earlier life to let you know that I understand what it means to feel hopeless and unloved. Years ago, God inspired me to share these truths in order to help set free other people who are in similar situations. Since the first release of this book, I have continued to hear from thousands of people who share that they need prayer and teaching in order to walk victoriously in the life God has planned for them. They testify that this book has helped them greatly.

Recently, the Lord encouraged me to expand the teaching in this book to further develop a solid foundation for people who are ready to let go of their past and to move on to the beautiful life God wants them to enjoy. Based on my own experiences, and the extensive studies I have done on behavioral addictions caused by abuse, I share how God's love will override negative results from past abuse. I also share insight on the two kinds of pain that an abused person must face, the pain of change or the pain of staying the same, and six steps to achieve emotional healing.

Running from the past does not lead to healing, so I identify several ways people run from the past so you can avoid delays in reaching your own victory. I will explain how to move forward through the doorways of pain that have become obstacles to the future.

If you need to let go of the past, and receive an inner strengthening from God that will enable you to trust others, develop and maintain intimate friendships, and enjoy your life again, then this book is for you. Once you begin, press on by reading through to the end of the book in order to reach the good news of the prize for which God has called you.

I know firsthand that God is a rewarder of those who diligently seek Him. You can learn how to shake off trouble and receive a double recompense for all you have been through.

PART ONE

I Once Was Bound

Some sat in darkness and in the shadow of death, being bound in affliction and in irons, because they had rebelled against the words of God and spurned the counsel of the Most High.

PSALM 107:10-11

1

Trophies of Grace

Many people appear to have their lives together outwardly, but inside they are emotional wrecks because they have been traumatized by abuse. A victim of trauma is someone who has been wounded physically or emotionally by some sudden or substantial shock that created severe and lasting damage to the psychological development of that individual.

I believe there are many traumatized people in the world who have been so abused in the past that they are psychologically deficient; they are unable to function normally in everyday life. There are people who have been through such trauma that it severely jarred their emotions, because they endured something that was so awful it was unspeakable.

Surviving the trauma of abuse can throw people into a state of psychological damage that prohibits them from functioning properly in relationships with others. Such victims do not understand what is wrong with them, or how to get out of their destructive behavior patterns so they can live a normal life. That was my situation before I learned how to gain the victory over the trauma in my life.

Through seeking God and reading His Word, I found that the Lord's main concern is our *inner* life, because that is where we enjoy His presence. Jesus said, "For behold, the kingdom of God *is within you* [in your hearts] *and* among you [surrounding you]" (Luke 17:21, emphasis mine).

This book is a summation of how God taught me to triumph through Christ over the tragedy of abuse in my life. After I had spent many years preaching His Word, God led me to 2 Corinthians 2:14: "But thanks be to God, Who in Christ always leads us in triumph [as trophies of Christ's victory] and through us spreads *and* makes evident the fragrance of the knowledge of God everywhere."

One Thanksgiving morning, a spirit of thankfulness began to rise up within me as I considered all that God had done for me. He spoke to my heart that day and said to me, "Joyce, you are a trophy of My grace, and you are helping Me get other trophies." Then I had a vision of a display case in heaven, filled with trophies. I understood that when someone wins trophies, it is because that person is a champion at what he or she does. If people have baseball, golf, or bowling trophies displayed in their homes, it is obvious that they have spent a lot of time developing their skill in that particular area.

God is the Champion at bringing people from a place of destruction to a place of total victory. As they reach that place of victory they become trophies of His grace, and they are set on display as a fragrant reminder of God's goodness. I share my testimony in this book to help those who are still in the process of becoming a trophy for God.

Through both tragedies and triumphs, I have learned that Jesus is my King, and He wants to be yours, too. The kingdom He desires to reign over is our inner life—our mind, will, emotions, desires, and thoughts. The Word teaches clearly that "the kingdom of God is not a matter of [getting the] food and drink [one likes], but instead it is righteousness (that state which makes a person acceptable to God) and [heart] peace and joy in the Holy Spirit. He who serves Christ in this way is acceptable *and* pleasing to God and is approved by men" (Romans 14:17-18).

In other words, if God's kingdom rules within us, we will enjoy righteousness, peace, and joy in the Holy Spirit. We will also be acceptable to God and approved by men. Jesus said that we should not worry about external things, such as food and clothes, but that we should "seek (aim at and strive after) first of all His kingdom and His righteousness (His way of doing and being right), and then all these things taken together will be given [us] besides" (Matthew 6:33).

Before all else, we are to seek the kingdom of God, *which is within us*, and then all of our external concerns will be taken care of. When we accept Jesus as our Lord, He rules our inner life and brings with Him righteousness, peace, and joy. No matter what difficulties or trials we may experience in our outward life, if we are whole inside, we will not only survive, we will enjoy our lives.

Our inner life with God is much more important than our outer life. Therefore, emotional healing, which I also refer to as inner healing, is a subject that needs to be discussed in a scriptural, balanced way that produces godly results. The apostle Paul said that we can be "assured that He Who raised up the Lord Jesus will raise us up also with Jesus and bring us . . . into His presence" (2 Corinthians 4:14). In verses 16-18 he continued:

> Therefore we do not become discouraged (utterly spiritless, exhausted, and wearied out through fear). Though our outer man is [progressively] decaying *and* wasting away, yet our inner self is being [progressively] renewed day after day.

> For our light, momentary affliction (this slight distress of the passing hour) is ever more and more abundantly preparing *and* producing *and* achieving for us an everlasting weight of glory [beyond all measure, excessively surpassing all comparisons and all calculations, a vast and transcendent glory and blessedness never to cease!],
>
> Since we consider *and* look not to the things that are seen but to the things that are unseen; for the things that are visible are temporal (brief and fleeting), but the things that are invisible are deathless *and* everlasting.

Everyone is subject to what Paul called, "momentary afflictions," and some of us have suffered what seemed at the time to be unbearable, emotional pain. But Jesus came "to announce release to the captives and recovery of sight to the blind, to send forth as delivered those who are oppressed [who are downtrodden, bruised, crushed, and broken down by calamity]" (Luke 4:18-19).

The King James Version of verse 18 says that Jesus said He came "to heal the brokenhearted." According to *Strong's Exhaustive Concordance,* the word translated *brokenhearted* in this verse is a combination of two Greek words, *kardia*, meaning simply "*heart*,"[1] and *suntribo* (*soon-tree'-bo*), which means "to *crush completely*, i.e. to *shatter* . . . break (in pieces), broken to shivers . . . , bruise."[2] I believe Jesus came to heal those who are broken inside—those who are crushed and wounded *inwardly*.

If you have been traumatized by abuse, it is my hope that this book will serve as a road map to get from the ashes of devastation to the beauty of health and wholeness in your inner self. I pray that you will find this message to be simple, clear, and powerful, and that the Holy Spirit will enable you to follow Him to your destination of peace and joy.

My prayer for you is paraphrased from Ephesians 3:16:

I pray that you will be strengthened in the inner man through the power of the Holy Spirit and that He will indwell your innermost being and personality.

I also encourage you to always remember God's promise, found in Hebrews 13:5-6:

> For He [God] Himself has said, I will not in any way fail you *nor* give you up *nor* leave you without support. [I will] not, [I will] not, [I will] not in any degree leave you helpless *nor* forsake *nor* let [you] down (relax My hold on you)! [Assuredly not!]
>
> So we take comfort *and* are encouraged *and* confidently *and* boldly say, The Lord is my Helper; I will not be seized with alarm [I will not fear or dread or be terrified]. What can man do to me?

2

The Ashes of Abuse

I BELIEVE THAT most people are abused in one way or another during their lifetime. Almost every person can remember a time when he felt mistreated. I also believe there are multitudes of people who have been severely traumatized by the abuse that has been inflicted upon them.

Some of the definitions of the verb *abuse* are: "to put to a wrong or improper use"; "DECEIVE"; "to use so as to injure or damage: MALTREAT"; "to attack in words: REVILE." Definitions for the noun *abuse* include: "a corrupt practice or custom"; "improper or excessive use or treatment: MISUSE"; "a deceitful act: DECEPTION"; "language that condemns or vilifies . . . unjustly, intemperately, and angrily"; "physical maltreatment."[3]

Some common forms of abuse are: physical, verbal, mental, emotional, and sexual. Any form of ongoing abuse can produce a root of rejection in the individual who has been mistreated, and this defensive sense of unworthiness can then cause major problems in the interpersonal relationships of that individual. Today we live in a society filled with people who do not know how to get along with other people; even though the abuse in their lives has stopped, the residue of trauma continues to affect their ability to relate to others.

God created us for love and acceptance, but the devil works hard to keep us feeling rejected because he knows that a lack of self-worth and root feelings of rejection injure individuals, families, and friendships.

The above-mentioned types of abuse—whether they take the form of broken relationships, abandonment, divorce, false accusations, exclusion from groups, dislike by teachers and other authority figures, ridicule by peers—or any one of hundreds of other such hurtful actions—can and do cause emotional wounds that can hinder people in their efforts to maintain healthy, lasting relationships.

Have You Been Abused?

If you have been treated wrongly or improperly, it can deeply affect your emotional state. But to be healed of the pain of abuse, you must *want* to get well.

One of my favorite passages of scriptures (but a startling one) is John, chapter 5. In verse 5, Jesus is described as seeing a man lying by the pool of Bethesda who had been sick with a deep-seated and lingering disease for thirty-eight years. Knowing how long this poor man had been in that terrible condition, Jesus asked him, "Do you want to become well? [Are you really in earnest about getting well?]" (v. 6).

What kind of a question is that to ask someone who has been hurting for that long? It is a proper question because not everyone wants to get well badly enough to do what is required. Wounded emotions can become a prison that locks self in and others out. But Jesus came to open prison doors and to set the captives free (see Luke 4:18-19).

This man at Bethesda, like so many people today, had a

deep-seated and lingering disorder for a long, long time. I am sure that after thirty-eight years he had learned how to function with his disorder. People who are in prison function, but they are not free. However, sometimes prisoners, whether physical or emotional, become so accustomed to being in bondage that they settle in with their condition and learn to live with it.

Are you an "emotional prisoner"? If so, how long have you been in that condition? Is it a deep-seated and lingering disorder? Do you want to be free of it? Do you really want to be well? Jesus wants to heal you. He is willing, are you?

Do You Want to Be Free and Well?

Gaining freedom from emotional bondage is not easy. I will be honest from the beginning and say, point blank, that for many, many people, getting free from the pain of the past will not be easy. This discussion may provoke feelings and emotions they have been trying to hide rather than facing them. You may be one of those people.

Perhaps you have experienced feelings and emotions in the past that have been too painful to deal with, so each time they have surfaced to your memory, you have said to God, "I am not ready yet, Lord! I will face that problem later!" This book will deal with the emotional pain caused by what others may have done to you, and also with your responsibility to God for overcoming those traumas in order to get well.

Some people (actually a great number of people) have a hard time accepting responsibility for their own emotional health. In these pages, we will deal in a practical way with forgiveness, repressed anger, self-pity, the chip-on-the-shoulder syndrome, the you-owe-me attitude, and many, many other poisonous attitudes that need cleansing if you are ever to be fully well.

You may think, *But who will deal with the person who hurt me?* We will get around to that issue too. You may also be wondering, *What makes this woman think that she is such an authority on the subject of emotions—especially mine?* You may have questions you would like to ask me, such as: "Do you have a degree in psychology? Where did you do your study? Have you been through any of the things I am going through? How do you know what it is like to be caught in an emotional prison?"

I have answers to all those questions, and if you are brave enough to face your situation and have determined that you really want to get well, then read on.

I Was Abused

My schooling, degrees, experience, and qualifications to teach on this subject come from personal experience. I always say, "I graduated from the school of life." I claim the words of the prophet Isaiah as my diploma:

> THE SPIRIT of the Lord God is upon me, because the Lord has anointed *and* qualified me to preach the Gospel *of* good tidings to the meek, the poor, *and* afflicted; He has sent me to bind up *and* heal the brokenhearted, to proclaim liberty to the [physical and spiritual] captives and the opening of the prison *and* of the eyes to those who are bound,
>
> To proclaim the acceptable year of the Lord [the year of His favor] and the day of vengeance of our God, to comfort all who mourn,
>
> To grant [consolation and joy] to those who mourn in Zion—*to give them an ornament (a garland or diadem) of*

> *beauty instead of ashes*, the oil of joy instead of mourning, the garment [expressive] of praise instead of a heavy, burdened, *and* failing spirit—that they may be called oaks of righteousness [lofty, strong, and magnificent, distinguished for uprightness, justice, and right standing with God], the planting of the Lord, that He may be glorified. (Isaiah 61:1-3 emphasis mine)

God has exchanged my ashes for beauty and has called me to help others to learn to allow Him to do the same for them.

I was sexually, physically, verbally, mentally, and emotionally abused from the time I can remember until I finally left home at the age of eighteen. Actually, several men abused me in my childhood. I have been rejected, abandoned, betrayed, and divorced. I know what it is to be an "emotional prisoner."

My purpose in writing this book is not to give my full testimony in detail, but to give you enough of my own experience so that you will believe that I know what it means to hurt. I can show you how to recover from the pain and trauma of abuse. I want to help you, and I can do that better if you truly believe that I understand what you are going through.[4]

Before I begin discussing the details of my childhood and sharing some of the things I experienced, I wish to say that in no way do I mean any of these things to be degrading to my parents. Since the first release of this book, God has been faithful to restore my relationship with them.

But I have learned that hurting people hurt people; that most people who hurt others have been hurt themselves by someone else. God has enabled me by His grace to say, "Father, forgive them, for they really did not know what they were doing."

I tell this story only for the purpose of helping others who, like me, were abused.

3

The Fellowship of Fear

BECAUSE OF THE sexual and emotional abuse I received at home, my entire childhood was filled with fear. My father controlled me with his anger and intimidation. He never physically forced me to submit to him, but I was so afraid of his anger that I did whatever he told me to do. He did force me to pretend that I liked what he was doing to me, and that I wanted him to do it.

The few times I timidly attempted to speak out in honesty about my situation were devastating. My father's violent reaction—his ranting and raving—was so frightening to me that I soon learned just to do whatever he said without objection. I believe that my inability to express my true feelings about what was happening to me, and my being forced to act as though I enjoyed the perverse things he did to me, left me with many deep-seated emotional wounds.

My father worked evenings and would come home around eleven or twelve at night. I can remember how my entire body would fill with fear as soon as I heard his key turning the lock. I would get stiff all over, because I never knew if he was going to come in my room and try to put his hands on me, or if he would come in mad about something he did not like.

One of the hardest things for me was the lack of stability of ever knowing what to expect; I lived with the fear of never knowing what I could and could not do. I could do one thing one day, and my father would be fine with it, but I could do the exact same thing a few days later and get slapped across the room for it.

Fear was my constant companion: fear of my father, fear of his anger, fear of being exposed, fear of my mother finding out what was happening, and fear of having friends.

My fear of having friends stemmed from two factors: If they were female, I was afraid that my father would attempt to draw them into his trap also. If they were male, I was afraid that my father would harm them, or me. He violently accused me of being sexually active with male acquaintances from school. He would not permit anyone to come near me because I "belonged" to him.

While in high school, I was never allowed to go to a football game, a baseball game, a basketball game. I tried to develop acquaintances at school, but I never allowed the relationships to ripen to the extent that I would be expected to invite my new friends to my house. I did not let anyone feel free to contact me at home. If the phone rang, and the call was for me, I would panic thinking, *What if it is someone from school?*

All the time I was dealing with a fear of having friends and of being lonely, I was still unwilling to involve anyone else in what was potentially a disaster for them, and one that would certainly cause me more embarrassment and shame.

FEAR! FEAR! FEAR!

My father drank heavily every weekend, often taking me with him on his drinking bouts and physically using me at his will. Many times, he would come home angry and beat up my mother. One time he beat her because he said her nose was big. He did not hit me very often, but I believe that watching him senselessly beating my mother was just as damaging as if he had been hitting me.

My father controlled everything that went on around him. He decided what time we got up and when we went to bed; what we ate, wore, and spent; with whom we associated; what we watched on television—in short, everything in our lives. He was verbally abusive both to my mother and to me, and eventually to my only brother, who was born when I was nine years old. I remember wanting so desperately for the new baby to be a girl. I thought that maybe if there was another female child in the family I might be left alone, at least part of the time.

My father cursed almost constantly, using extremely vulgar and filthy language. He was critical of everything and everybody. It was his opinion that none of us ever did anything right, or that we would ever amount to anything worthwhile. Most of the time, we were reminded that we were "just no good."

At times my father would be just the opposite. He would give us money and tell us to go shopping; sometimes he even bought us presents. He was manipulative and coercive. He did whatever he needed to do in order to get what he wanted. Other people had no value to him at all except to use for his own selfish purposes.

There was no peace in our home. I actually did not know what real peace was until I was grown and had been immersed in the Word of God for many years.

I was born-again at the age of nine while visiting relatives out of town. One night I went with them to attend a church service, intent on finding salvation. I do not even know how I knew I needed to be saved, except that God must have placed that desire within my heart. I did receive Jesus Christ as my Savior that evening and experienced a glorious cleansing. Before that moment I had always felt dirty because of the incest. Now, for the first time, I felt clean, as though I had received an inner bath. However, since the problem did not go away, once I returned home my old feelings returned. I thought that I had lost Jesus, so I never knew any real inner peace and joy.

The Betrayal

What about my mother? Where did she fit into all this? Why didn't she help me? I was about eight or nine years old when I told my mother what was going on between my father and me. She examined me and confronted my dad, but he claimed that I was lying—and she chose to believe him rather than me. What woman would not want to believe her husband in such a situation? I think that way down deep inside, my mother knew the truth. She just hoped against hope that she was wrong.

When I was fourteen years old, she walked into the house one day, having returned earlier than expected from grocery shopping, and actually caught my father in the act of sexually abusing me. She looked, walked out, and came back two hours later, acting as if she had never been there.

My mother betrayed me.

She did not help me, and she should have.

Many, many years later (actually thirty years later), she confessed to me that she just could not bring herself to face the scandal. She had never mentioned it for thirty years! During that time period she had suffered a nervous breakdown. Everyone who knew her blamed it on "the change of life."

For two years she underwent shock treatments, which temporarily erased portions of her memory. None of the doctors knew what they were helping her forget, but they all agreed that she needed to forget something. It was obvious there was something on her mind that was eating away at her mental health.

My mother claimed that her problem was caused by her physical condition. She had an exceptionally hard time during that period of her life due to severe female problems at an earlier age. Following a complete hysterectomy at age thirty-six, she was thrown into premature menopause. At the time, most doctors did not believe in giving hormones to women, so this was a very difficult time for her. It seems that everything in her life was more than she was able to handle.

Personally, I will always believe that my mother's emotional collapse was the result of the years of abuse she had endured, and the truth that she refused to face and deal with. Remember, in John 8:32 our Lord told us: "You will know the Truth, and the Truth will set you free."

God's Word is truth, and, if applied, has inherent power to set a captive free. God's Word also brings us face to face with the issues of our lives. If we choose to turn and run away when the Lord says to stand and confront, we will stay in bondage.

Leaving Home

At age eighteen, I moved away from home while my father was at work. Shortly thereafter, I married the first young man who showed an interest in me.

Like me, my new husband had lots of problems. He was a

manipulator, a thief, and a con man. Most of the time, he did not even work. We moved around a lot, and once he abandoned me in California with nothing but one dime and a carton of soda pop bottles. I was afraid, but since I was accustomed to fear and trauma, I was probably not as affected as someone with less "experience" would have been.

My husband also abandoned me several times simply by leaving during the day while I was at work. Each time he left, he would be gone anywhere from a few weeks to several months. Then he would suddenly reappear, and I would listen to his sweet talk and apologies and take him back—only to have the same thing happen all over again. When he was with me, he drank constantly and had relationships with other women regularly.

For five years we played at what we called a marriage. We were both so young, only eighteen, and neither of us had had proper parenting. We were completely ill-equipped to help one another. My problems were only complicated more following a miscarriage at the age of twenty-one and the birth of my oldest son when I was twenty-two. This event took place during the final year of our marriage. My husband left me and moved in with another woman who lived two blocks from our place, telling anyone who would listen that the child I was carrying was not his.

I remember coming dangerously close to losing my mind during that summer of 1965. Throughout my pregnancy, I lost weight because I could not eat. Without friends, money, or insurance, I went through a hospital clinic, seeing a different doctor each time I had a checkup. Actually, the doctors I saw were interns in training. I was unable to sleep, so I began taking over-the-counter sleeping pills. Thank God, they did not harm my unborn child or me.

The temperature that summer rose to more than a hundred degrees, and there was no fan or air-conditioning in my third-floor, attic apartment. My only material possession was an old Studebaker automobile that got vapor locked on a regular basis. Since my father had always insisted that some day I would need his help and come crawling back to him, I was determined to do anything but that—even though I did not know what it would be.

I can remember being under such mental strain that I would sit and stare at the walls or out the window for hours, not even realizing what I was doing. I worked until my baby was due. When I had to quit my job, my hairdresser and her mother took me in.

My baby was four and a half weeks late. I had no idea what to expect, and no notion of how to care for him when he was born. When the baby did come, my husband showed up at the hospital. Since the baby looked so much like him, there was no way he could deny that it was his. Once again he said he was sorry and that he was going to change.

When it was time for me to be discharged from the hospital, we had no place to live, so my husband contacted his brother's ex-wife, who was a wonderful Christian woman, and she let us live with her for a while until I was able to go back to work.

I think you can imagine from these few details what my life was like. Actually, it was ridiculous! There was nothing stable in my entire existence, and stability was something that I needed and craved desperately.

Finally, in the summer of 1966, I reached the point of not caring what happened to me. I could not stand the thought of staying with my husband any longer. I did not have one ounce of respect for the man, especially since, to top it all off, by this time he was in trouble with the law. I took my son and what I could carry and walked out. I went to a corner phone booth where I called my dad and asked him if I could come home. Of course, he was delighted!

After I had lived at home for a couple of months, I learned that my divorce had been granted. That was in September of 1966. By that time my mother's mental health was growing worse by the day. She had begun to have violent fits, accusing store clerks of robbing her, threatening the people she worked with over meaningless details. She even started carrying a knife in her purse. She ranted and raved about anything and everything. I distinctly remember one night when she beat me with a broom because I had failed to mop the bathroom floor! While all this was going on, I made an occupation of steering clear of my father. As much as possible, I avoided being left alone with him.

In short, my life was a living hell.

For "entertainment," I began to go to bars on weekends. I suppose I was looking for someone to love me. I would have a few drinks, but rarely ever enough to get drunk. I really had never cared much for drinking. I also refused to sleep with the various men I met. Even though my life was a mess, there was a deep desire in me to be good and pure.

Confused, afraid, lonely, discouraged, and depressed, I often prayed, "Dear God, please let me be happy . . . some day. Give me someone who will really love me—and make it someone who will take me to church."

My Knight in Shining Armor

My parents owned and resided in a two-family apartment. One of their renters worked with a man named Dave Meyer. One evening Dave came by to pick up his friend to go bowling. I was washing my mother's car. He saw me and tried to flirt with me, but I was my usual sarcastic self. He asked me if I wanted to wash his car when I was finished with mine, and I replied, "If you want your car washed, wash it yourself!" Because of my experience with my father and my former husband, I did not trust men at all, and that is an understatement!

Dave, however, was being led by the Spirit of God. Born-again and baptized in the Holy Spirit, he loved God with all his heart. At twenty-six years of age, he was also ready to get married and had been praying for six months that God would lead him to the right woman. He had even asked the Lord for her to be someone who needed help!

Since Dave was being led by the Lord, my sarcasm only served to encourage him, instead of insulting him. Later he told his friend from work that he would like to have a date with me. At first I refused, but later I changed my mind. We had been out on five dates when Dave asked me to marry him. He told me that he had known the first night we went out together that he wanted me to be his wife, but that he had decided to wait a few weeks before proposing marriage, lest he frighten me.

For my part, I certainly did not know what love was, and was not eager to get involved with another man. However, since things were getting even worse at home, and since I was living in total panic all the time, I decided that anything would be better than what I was going through at the moment.

Dave asked me if I would go to church with him, which I was willing to do. Remember, one of my prayer requests had been that when the Lord gave me someone to love me, he would be a person who would take me to church. I strongly desired to live a Christian life, but I knew that I needed someone strong to lead the way. Dave also promised to be good to my little boy, who was ten months old when we met. I had named him David, which was what my brother was called and was my favorite name for a boy. I am still amazed at the way the Lord was working out a plan for my good, right in the midst of my darkest despair.

Dave and I were married on January 7, 1967, but we did not

live "happily ever after"! Marriage did not solve my problems, and neither did going to church. My problems were not in my home life or my marriage, but in me, in my wounded, crippled emotions.

Abuse leaves a person emotionally handicapped, unable to maintain healthy, lasting relationships without some kind of intervention. I wanted to give and receive love, but I could not. Like my father, I was controlling, manipulative, angry, critical, negative, overbearing, and judgmental. All that I had grown up with, I had become. Filled with self-pity, I was verbally abusive, depressed, and bitter. I could go on and on describing my personality, but I am sure you get the picture.

I functioned in society. I worked; Dave worked. We went to church together. We got along part of the time, only then because Dave was extremely easygoing. He usually let me have my way, but when he didn't it made me mad. As far as I was concerned, I was right about everything. To me, I did not have a problem; everyone else did.

Now remember, I was born-again. I loved Jesus. I believed that my sins were forgiven and that I would go to heaven when I died. But I knew no victory, no peace, no joy in my everyday life. Although I believed that Christians were supposed to be happy, I certainly was not! I did not even know what righteousness, imputed through the blood of Jesus, was. I felt condemned all the time. I was out of control. The only time I did not hate myself was when I was working toward some personal goal which I thought would provide me a sense of self-worth.

I kept thinking that if *things* would change, if other *people* would change, then I would be all right. If my husband, my kids, my finances, my health, were different; if I could go on vacation, get a new car, buy a new dress; if I could get out of the house, find a job, earn more money, then I would be happy and fulfilled. I was always doing what is described in Jeremiah 2:13—I was digging wells that had no water in them.

I was making the frustrating, tragic mistake of trying to find the kingdom of God, which is righteousness, peace, and joy (see Romans 14:17), in things and other people. What I did not realize is that the kingdom of God is within us, as the apostle Paul explained: "which is Christ within *and* among you, the Hope of [realizing the] glory" (Colossians 1:27). Jesus said, "For behold, *the kingdom of God is within you [in your hearts] and* among you [surrounding you]" (Luke 17:21, emphasis mine). My joy had to be found in Christ, but it took me years and years to find that out.

I tried to earn righteousness by being good, through works of the flesh. I was on the evangelism committee and the church board. My husband was an elder in the church. Our children went to parochial school. I tried to do all the right things. I tried and tried and tried, and yet it seemed that I just could not keep myself from making mistakes. I was worn out, burned out, frustrated, and miserable!

I Was Sincerely Ignorant of the Problem

It never occurred to me that I was suffering from the years of abuse and rejection I had gone through. I thought that all that was behind me. It was true that it was no longer happening to me physically, but it was all recorded in my emotions and in my mind. I still felt the effects of it, and I still acted them out.

I needed emotional healing!

Legally, I was a new creature in Christ. The Word says, "Therefore if any person is [ingrafted] in Christ (the Messiah) he is a new creation (a new creature altogether); the old [previous moral and spiritual condition] has passed away. Behold, the fresh *and* new has come!" (2 Corinthians 5:17). But experientially, I had not yet taken hold of the new creation reality. I lived out of my own mind, will, and emotions, which were all damaged. Jesus had paid the price for my total deliverance, but I had no idea how to receive His gracious gift.

4

Behavior Addictions Caused by Abuse

THE FIRST THING to realize is that the fruit in our lives (our behavior) comes from somewhere. A person who is violent is that way for a reason; bad behavior is like bad fruit of a bad tree with bad roots. *Rotten fruit comes from rotten roots; good fruit comes from good roots.*

It is important to take a close look at your roots. If they are unpleasant, harmful, or abusive, the good news is that you can be uprooted from that bad soil and be transplanted into the good soil of Christ Jesus. You can be rooted and grounded in Him and in His love: "May Christ through your faith [actually] dwell (settle down, abide, make His permanent home) in your hearts! May you be rooted deep in love *and* founded securely on love, that you may have the power *and* be strong to apprehend *and* grasp with all the saints [God's devoted people, the experience of that love] what is the breadth and length and height and depth [of it]" (Ephesians 3:17-18).

The Word teaches: "Have the roots [of your being] firmly *and* deeply planted [in Him, fixed and founded in Him], being continually built up in Him, becoming increasingly more confirmed *and* established in the faith, just as you were taught, and abounding *and* overflowing in it with thanksgiving" (Colossians 2:7).

Jesus will graft you into Himself. As you, a branch, are grafted into Him, Who is the Vine (see John 15:5), you will begin to receive all the "sap" (the riches of His love and grace), which flow from Him. In other words, if while you were growing up you did not receive what you needed to make you sound and healthy, Jesus will gladly give it to you now.

In my own life there was a lot of bad fruit, which I kept trying to get rid of. I worked hard at trying to behave correctly. Yet it seemed that no matter what kind of bad behaviors I tried to get rid of, two or three others popped up somewhere else. It was like trying to get rid of dandelion weeds. I kept pulling off the visible part, but I was not getting to the hidden root of the problem. The root was alive and kept producing a new crop of problems.

As the following illustrations reveal, rotten roots yield rotten fruit, but good fruit comes from good roots.

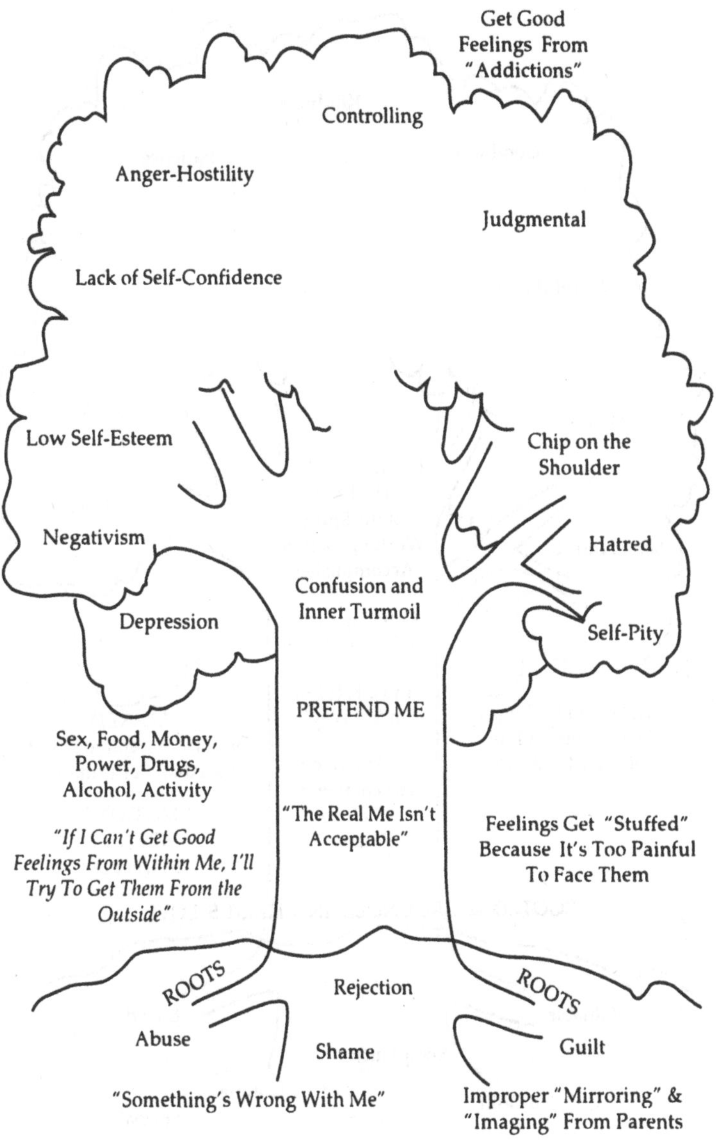
Get Good
Feelings From
"Addictions"
Controlling
Anger-Hostility
Judgmental
Lack of Self-Confidence
Low Self-Esteem
Chip on the
Shoulder
Negativism
Hatred
Confusion and
Inner Turmoil
Depression
Self-Pity
PRETEND ME
Sex, Food, Money,
Power, Drugs,
Alcohol, Activity
*"If I Can't Get Good
Feelings From Within Me, I'll
Try To Get Them From the
Outside"*
"The Real Me Isn't
Acceptable"
Feelings Get "Stuffed"
Because It's Too Painful
To Face Them
ROOTS
Rejection
ROOTS
Abuse
Shame
Guilt
"Something's Wrong With Me"
Improper "Mirroring" &
"Imaging" From Parents

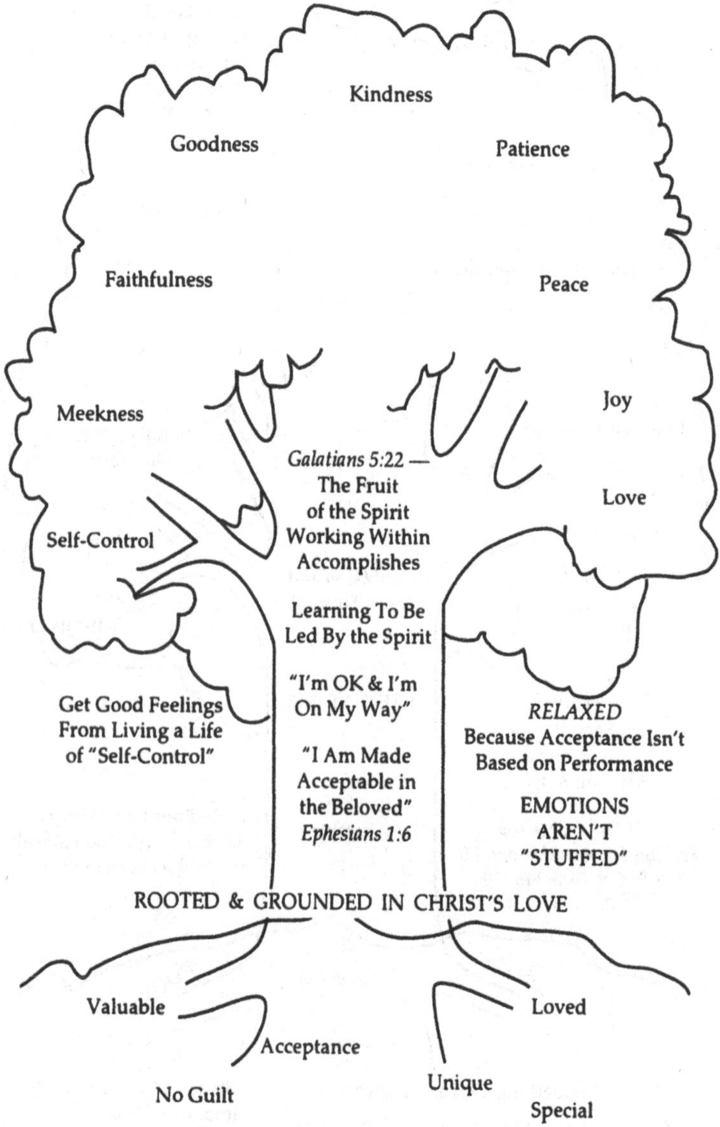
Kindness
Goodness
Patience
Faithfulness
Peace
Joy
Meekness
Love
Self-Control
Galatians 5:22 —
The Fruit
of the Spirit
Working Within
Accomplishes
Learning To Be
Led By the Spirit
"I'm OK & I'm
On My Way"
"I Am Made
Acceptable in
the Beloved"
Ephesians 1:6
Get Good Feelings
From Living a Life
of "Self-Control"
RELAXED
Because Acceptance Isn't
Based on Performance
EMOTIONS
AREN'T
"STUFFED"
ROOTED & GROUNDED IN CHRIST'S LOVE
Valuable
Loved
Acceptance
Unique
No Guilt
Special

As an illustration, the Lord gave me this example. Have you ever noticed a foul odor when you opened the refrigerator door? You immediately knew that there was something spoiled in there, but in order to find out what was causing the smell, you had to remove everything in the refrigerator.

The same principle applies to your personal life. If you are having emotional problems, it may be because there is something spoiled deep within you. You may have to do some searching, some emptying out, and even some taking apart in order to get to the source of the problem and remove it so that everything can be made fresh and new.

Remember, uprooting can be traumatic and painful. Being replanted, becoming rooted and grounded, is a process that takes time. It is by faith and patience that we inherit God's promises (see Hebrews 6:12), so be patient.

God is the Author and the Finisher (see Hebrews 12:2 KJV). He will finish what He has begun in you: "And I am convinced *and* sure of this very thing, that He Who began a good work in you will continue until the day of Jesus Christ [right up to the time of His return], developing [that good work] *and* perfecting *and* bringing it to full completion in you" (Philippians 1:6).

BAD FRUIT

I had so much bad fruit in my life that I experienced regular bouts of depression, negativism, self-pity, quick temper, and the chip-on-the-shoulder syndrome. I had a controlling, domineering spirit. I was harsh, hard, rigid, legalistic, and judgmental. I held grudges and was fearful—especially of being rejected.

I was one person on the inside and another on the outside. I pretended to be confident, and in some ways I was. Still, I had low self-esteem. My so-called confidence was not really based on who I was in Christ, but on the approval of others, on my appearance and accomplishments, and on other such external factors. Many people think they are confident, but if their superficial exterior is stripped away, they are actually scared stiff! I was confused and full of inner turmoil.

I am extremely blessed to be able to say that I never became addicted to drugs or alcohol. I smoked cigarettes, but had no other chemical dependencies. I just plain did not like alcohol. I would take a few drinks, but as soon as I started feeling woozy, I would never drink beyond that point.

I always had a lot of self-control. It was part of my personality not to let anything control me, so I stayed away from drugs. I think the fact that my father had controlled my life so long fostered a determination in me that nothing else would. Although I could not control my inner problems, I seemed to have wisdom about staying away from things that could render me dependent upon them.

I took diet pills once because I was always about twenty-five pounds overweight. Although a doctor prescribed them for me, they made me high. They were amphetamines, but I had no idea they were harmful. I loved the way they made me feel all day! When I was on them, I could work like a machine, clean house, be creative and friendly; I was up, up, up. But when they wore off, I was worn out!

Although I did not lose any weight, the pills did take care of my appetite—until they wore off. I would not eat all day, but at night I would feel so down that I would make up for what I had missed throughout the day. I remember debating about whether I should get the prescription refilled, but I *knew* inside that I would get addicted to the pills if I kept taking them, so I just quit.

I realize now that the ability to avoid things that could have destroyed me came as a result of having received Jesus when I was nine years old. Even though I did not know how to develop a real relationship with the Lord, He was always with me and was helping me in ways I did not recognize at the time for lack of knowledge. Years later, these blessings were made clear to me.

I know that God's grace and mercy kept me from serious problems such as crime, drugs, alcoholism, and prostitution. I am grateful to the Lord and still in awe of how He kept me. Although I did not have those kinds of problems, I had plenty of others. Bad roots had caused my bad fruit.

PRETENDING

I was so miserable and unhappy. Yet, like so many people, I pretended that everything was fine. We human beings pretend for the benefit of others, not wanting them to know about our misery, but we also pretend for ourselves so that we do not have to face and deal with difficult issues.

I do not think I ever realized just how miserable I really was until I had spent some time in the Word of God and had begun to experience some emotional healing. If a person has never known true happiness, how can he know what he is missing? I do not remember ever being fully relaxed and truly happy as a child. I do not believe that anyone can enjoy life while living in constant fear.

I recall Dave talking about his childhood one evening after we were married. He grew up with seven brothers and sisters. They had so much love in their home and a lot of fun as children. Their summers were spent in the country with picnics, ball games, friends, and a Christian mother who played with them and taught them about Jesus. They did not have much money because Dave's father had died from liver disease brought on by alcoholism. Yet the influence, prayers, and Christian example of Dave's mother kept the family out of trouble. *They had love, which is what all of us need and are actually created for.*

As Dave shared with me that evening about all the good times he and his family had and how much he enjoyed his youthful years, I suddenly had a realization that I did not like. I could never, ever remember being happy as a child! Something had been stolen from me that I could never get back. I felt terribly cheated. Perhaps you feel the same way. If so, God will do for you what He has done for me. He will make it up to you. He will, Himself, be your reward and will recompense you for what you have lost.

I realized that I had to stop pretending and face the truth. I had some addictive behaviors from my past. That past was not Dave's fault, nor my children's fault. It was unfair to continue making them suffer for something in which they had had no part.

Addictive Behaviors

Addictive behaviors that can develop from abuse are probably endless, but here is a partial list:

- ❖Substance abuse
  - Alcohol
  - Drugs (illegal and prescription)
- ❖Monetary obsessions
  - Excessive spending
  - Hoarding
- ❖Food disorders
  - Bulimia (binge-purge)
  - Anorexia (self-starvation)
  - Obesity caused by gluttony

Note: Some people who have been promiscuous stay overweight on purpose in order to avoid being attractive. They fear falling back into temptation. Those who have been deprived of love may eat to make up to themselves for what they have missed.

❖Feeling addictions
- Rage
- Sadness
- Fear
- Excessive excitement
- Religious righteousness
- Joy fixation (wearing a continuous, frozen smile; never appearing to be angry; laughing at inappropriate times; speaking only of happy things)

❖Thought addictions
- Excessive detailing
- Worry
- Nonstop talking
- Lustful thoughts
- Unsettled mind (never at rest; always figuring out what to say and do, how to react, etc.)

❖Activity obsessions
- Work
- Sports
- Reading
- Gambling
- Exercise
- Television viewing
- Owning and caring for excessive numbers of pets

❖Will addictions
- Controlling—Controlling people feel they must have their way in every situation. They cannot submit emotion

to logic or reason. They feel safe only when they are in control.

- Controlled—Those controlled become so passive, they give their will over to people and do whatever anyone says. They can even become possessed or severely oppressed by giving their will to the devil. They are so shame-based they feel they deserve nothing—not even choice.
- Reenactment addicts—These addicts reenact their own abuse on their children or repeatedly put themselves in situations as adults that produce the same type of thing that happened to them as a child. A similar scene gives flashbacks, and they take on the role of the abuser so as not to feel the painful memories of abuse. For example, a man who was beaten by his father in childhood may physically abuse his own children. He does this as a result of seeing flashbacks of the old scene and assuming the role of abuser, rather than waiting to be abused himself. A woman who was physically, sexually, or verbally abused by her father may marry a man, or even several men in succession, who will treat her in the same way. She may feel she is not worthy of anything else or that she deserves being mistreated. She may even see to it that she receives her mistreatment, perhaps even provoking the one who will abuse her.
- Caretaker—Some people find their worth in caring for others who need them. They feel so worthless that they become addicted to caretaking, helping, pleasing people, and being nice because doing so makes them feel good.

Created to Feel Good Inside

As human beings we are created by God to be happy and to feel good (right) about ourselves. As a matter of fact, we must feel good about ourselves or eventually we will develop some sort of uncontrolled behavior, because such behavior gives us "good feelings," even if only for a little while.

Think about this: A person addicted to drugs probably got started because his pain was so intense he felt compelled to get rid of it and feel good (high), even if only temporarily. The same thing is prevalent with drinking.

Many people use food as a comfort. Eating is enjoyable; it makes them feel good while they are engaging in it. Many people who have eating disorders are starving for love. They want to feel good about themselves. If they do not get good feelings from the inside, then they will get them from somewhere else.

If you have any addictive behaviors, this chapter may help you to understand the root of the problem. You can spend your entire life trying to subdue the outward behavior (the bad fruit), but it will come out somewhere else if the root has not been taken care of.

5

Rescued by Love

IF YOU ARE a person who has been abused, by now you have probably identified some problem areas in your life. To point out problems without offering a solution to them would be disastrous. If I did that, you would end up more frustrated than you were before you began reading this book.

I intend to outline the major truths that brought healing in my own life. As I do so, I would like to remind you that God is no respecter of persons (see Acts 10:34). What He does for one person, He will do for another, if it is a promise found in His Word.

The Process of Healing

My first husband did not know how to love, so I received no love at all from our relationship. Although my wonderful second husband, Dave, did truly love me, I knew no more than I ever had about how to receive love. I bounced back and forth between: (1) rejecting his love and closing him out of my life by building walls around myself to ensure that I would not get hurt (or so I thought), and, (2) trying to get him to love me with a kind of perfect and complete love that was humanly impossible for him to achieve.

In 1 John 4:18 we read that perfect love casts out fear. Only God can love perfectly and without fault. No matter how much anyone may love another person, he is still human. As our Lord said, "The spirit indeed is willing, but the flesh is weak" (Matthew 26:41). People always disappoint other people—they always love somewhat imperfectly, simply because that is part of human nature.

I was trying to get Dave to give me something that only God could give me, which was a sense of my own value and worth. I wanted my husband to love me totally and to treat me perfectly so I could finally feel good about myself. Whenever he failed me, disappointed me, or hurt me, I would put up walls between us and not allow him in at all for days or even weeks.

Many people who come from abusive, dysfunctional backgrounds cannot maintain healthy, lasting relationships because either they do not know how to receive love or they place an unbalanced demand on their marriage partners to give them what only God can give. The resulting frustration often ruins the marriage.

This same principle can be applied to friendships. One time a woman came up to me in a prayer line and said: "Joyce, help me. I am so lonely. Every time I get a friend, I suffocate her." This lady was so love-starved that if she found anyone who would pay any attention to her at all, she tried to collect all her past emotional debts from that individual, who owed her nothing. Her new friend was usually frightened away.

God's Boundless, Unconditional, Perfect Love

One day as I was reading the Bible, I noticed this statement in 2 Corinthians 5:7: "For we walk by faith [we regulate our lives and conduct ourselves by our conviction or belief respecting man's relationship to God and divine things, with trust and holy fervor; thus we walk] not by sight *or* appearance."

The Holy Spirit stopped me and asked, "What do you believe, Joyce, about your relationship with God? Do you believe He loves you?"

As I honestly began to search my heart and to study the Word of God on this subject, I came to the conclusion that I did believe that God loved me, but conditionally.

The Bible teaches us that God loves us perfectly or unconditionally. His perfect love for us is not based on our perfection. It is not based on anything except Himself. God is love (see 1 John 4:8). Love is not His occupation; it is Who He is. God always loves us, but often we stop receiving His love, especially if our behavior is not good.

I would like to stop here and present several passages of scripture that have come to mean a lot to me. Please take time to read them slowly. Digest them and allow them to become a part of you:

> And we know (understand, recognize, are conscious of, by observation and by experience) and believe (adhere to and put faith in and rely on) the love God cherishes for us. God is love, and he who dwells *and* continues in love dwells *and* continues in God, and God dwells *and* continues in him.
>
> In this [union and communion with Him] love is brought to completion *and* attains perfection with us, that we may have confidence for the day of judgment [with as-

surance and boldness to face Him], because as He is, so are we in this world.

There is no fear in love [dread does not exist], but full-grown (complete, perfect) love turns fear out of doors *and* expels every trace of terror! For fear brings with it the thought of punishment, and [so] he who is afraid has not reached the full maturity of love [is not yet grown into love's complete perfection].

We love *Him*, because He first loved us. (1 John 4:16-19)

In this the love of God was made manifest (displayed) where we are concerned: in that God sent His Son, the only begotten *or* unique [Son], into the world so that we might live through Him.

In this is love: not that we loved God, but that He loved us and sent His Son to be the propitiation (the atoning sacrifice) for our sins.

Beloved, if God loved us so [very much], we also ought to love one another. (1 John 4:9-11)

Who shall ever separate us from Christ's love? Shall suffering *and* affliction *and* tribulation? Or calamity *and* distress? Or persecution or hunger or destitution or peril or sword? (Romans 8:35)

For I am persuaded beyond doubt (am sure) that neither death nor life, nor angels nor principalities, nor things impending *and* threatening nor things to come, nor powers,

Nor height nor depth, nor anything else in all creation will be able to separate us from the love of God which is in Christ Jesus our Lord. (Romans 8:38-39)

> May Christ through your faith [actually] dwell (settle down, abide, make His permanent home) in your hearts! May you be rooted deep in love *and* founded securely on love,
>
> That you may have the power *and* be strong to apprehend and grasp with all the saints [God's devoted people, the experience of that love] what is the breadth and length and height and depth [of it];
>
> [That you may really come] to know [practically, through experience for yourselves] the love of Christ, which far surpasses mere knowledge [without experience]; that you may be filled [through all your being] unto all the fullness of God [may have the richest measure of the divine Presence, and become a body wholly filled and flooded with God Himself]! (Ephesians 3:17-19)

> Such hope never disappoints *or* deludes *or* shames us, for God's love has been poured out in our hearts through the Holy Spirit Who has been given to us. (Romans 5:5)

> Behold, I have indelibly imprinted (tattooed a picture of) you on the palm of each of My hands. (Isaiah 49:16)

First John 4:16 is a key scripture for me because it says that *we should be conscious and aware of God's love and put faith in it*. I was unconscious and unaware of God's love; therefore, I was not putting faith in His love for me.

When the devil condemned me, I did not know how to say, "Yes, I made a mistake," then go to God, ask for His forgiveness, receive His love, and press on. Instead, I would spend hours and even days feeling guilty about each little thing I did wrong. I was literally tormented! John tells us that fear has torment, but that the perfect love of God casts out fear (see 1

John 4:18). God's love for me was perfect because it was based on Him, not on me. So even when I failed, He kept loving me.

God's love for you is perfect—and unconditional. When you fail, He keeps on loving you, because His love is not based on you but on Him. When you fail, do you stop receiving God's love and start punishing yourself by feeling guilty and condemned? I felt guilty and bad about myself for the first forty years of my life. I faithfully carried my sack of guilt on my back everywhere I went. It was a heavy burden, and it was always with me. I made mistakes regularly, and I felt guilty about each one of them.

In Romans 8:33-35 the apostle Paul says:

> Who shall bring any charge against God's elect [when it is] God Who justifies [that is, Who puts us in right relation to Himself? Who shall come forward and accuse or impeach those whom God has chosen? Will God, Who acquits us?]
>
> Who is there to condemn [us]? Will Christ Jesus (the Messiah), Who died, or rather Who was raised from the dead, Who is at the right hand of God actually pleading *as* He intercedes for us?
>
> Who shall ever separate us from Christ's love?

The devil's goal is to separate us from God's love, because God's love is the main factor in our emotional healing.

We are created for love. In Ephesians 2:4-6 Paul says that God is so rich in mercy that He saved us and gave us what we do not deserve, in order to satisfy the demands of His intense love for us. Think about it. God intends to love us. He has to love us—He is love!

You and I are created for love! Sin separated us from God, but He loved us so much that He sent His only Son, Jesus, to die for us, to redeem us, to purchase us back, so that He could lavish His great love upon us. All we need to do is believe what the Bible says about our relationship with God. Once we do that, the healing process can begin.

During the first year that my husband Dave and I began our ministry called Life In The Word, the Holy Spirit worked with me to teach me about God's love. I kept a book of remembrance of special things the Lord did for me during that time—little things mostly, personal things that showed me that God cared. By this method I began to become more conscious of His unconditional love. It helped me to remember that God loved me.

If you can believe that God, Who is so perfect, loves you, then you can believe that you are worth loving.

Once you believe that you are accepted and loved by God, then you can begin accepting and loving yourself. Then not only will you start loving God in return, you will also start loving other people.

You Can't Give Away What You Don't Have!

Many people receive Jesus and then immediately start trying to love everybody. Too often they end up feeling condemned because they find that they just cannot do it. It is impossible to truly love others without first receiving the love of God, because there is no love there to give.

In 1 Corinthians, chapter 13, often called "the love chapter," Paul emphasizes this truth quite clearly. In the first verse he defines *love* as "(that reasoning, intentional, spiritual devotion such as is inspired by God's love for and in us)." This entire chapter is focused on teaching us how to walk in love, yet it clearly says that love must first be *in* us.

Most people can believe that God loves them when they can

feel that they deserve it. Problems arise when they feel that they do not deserve God's love, and yet desperately need it.

The following charts illustrate the ongoing effects of receiving or not receiving the love of God. Notice that the belief that God's love for us depends on our worthiness is a deception that causes many problems in our lives. On the other hand, believing that God loves us unconditionally brings much joy and blessedness.

Receiving God's Love

Determine in your heart that you will receive God's love. Here are some practical suggestions to help you do that. These are all things that I believe the Lord led me to do, and I believe they will be of help to you too. However, remember that we are all special and unique and that God has an individual, personalized plan for each of us. *Don't get lost in methods.*

The Trickle-Down Theory of Unconditional Love

Jesus loves me, this I know.
He loves me unconditionally.
THEREFORE: His love for me is based on Who *HE* is.
THEREFORE: I have not earned His love, nor can I earn His love.
THEREFORE: I cannot be separated from His love.
When I obey Him, He will bless me.
When I disobey Him, there will be consequences for my behavior.
He may not like my behavior, but He always loves me.
THEREFORE: Since I have experienced God's love, I know I am lovable.

THEREFORE, since I know that God loves me, I am able to believe that there are people who could love me too.

THEREFORE, I am able to trust people who genuinely love me.

THEREFORE, I am able to accept the love that those people give to me.

THEREFORE, since my most basic need for love and a sense of self-worth has been met by God, I don't need to be "fixed" by other people.

THEREFORE, although I have needs that I look to other people to meet (i.e., companionship, affection, fun), I believe those needs are balanced and God-given. I try to be honest in assessing those needs and in asking for what I need.

THEREFORE, I expect other people to be honest with me. I can handle criticism or confrontation, if it is done with love.

THEREFORE, since I know that I am God's special and unique creation, I know that the love I have to give is valuable.

THEREFORE, I do not feel that I have to "perform" for other people. Either they will love me for who I am, or they won't. It is important for me to be loved for who I am.

THEREFORE, I am able to get my mind off of what others are thinking *ABOUT ME* and focus on other people and *THEIR NEEDS*.

THEREFORE, I am able to sustain a healthy, loving, lasting relationship.

The Trickle-Down Theory of Conditional Love

Jesus loves me, but . . .
He loves me conditionally.
THEREFORE: His love is based on my performance.
THEREFORE: I have to earn His love by pleasing Him.
THEREFORE: When I please Him, I feel loved.
When I do not please Him, I feel rejected.
THEREFORE: If God, Who is "all-loving," does not always love, accept, and value me, how can I be expected to believe that I am valuable and lovable?
THEREFORE: I do not believe that I am basically a lovable, valuable person.

THEREFORE, I am not able to trust other people who say they love me. I suspect their motives or figure that they just do not know the "real" me yet.

THEREFORE, I cannot accept love from other people. I deflect it. I try to prove that I am right–that I am NOT lovable, and that they will eventually reject me.
THEREFORE, they usually do.

THEREFORE, I use the world's standards (money, status, clothes, etc.) to prove to others and myself that I am *VALUABLE*. I need strokes and feedback from other people to prove to myself and to others that I am *LOVABLE*.

THEREFORE, I need a "fresh fix" of strokes every day just to get through the day feeling good about myself.

THEREFORE, I look to others to give me something that only God can give me—a sense of my own *SELF-WORTH*.

THEREFORE, I place impossible demands on people who love me. I frustrate them. I am never satisfied with what they are giving me. I do not allow them to be honest with me or confront me. I am focused on me, and I expect them to be focused on me too.

THEREFORE, since I do not love who I *AM*, I do not expect that others will love me either. Why would anyone want something that has no real value?

THEREFORE, I try to earn their love by what I *DO*. I do not give out of a desire to love, but to *BE LOVED*. Most of what I do is tied up in "self," so the people I profess to love do not really feel loved. They feel manipulated. I am trying to avoid rejection rather than trying to build a loving relationship.

THEREFORE, I am not able to sustain a healthy, loving, lasting relationship.

These are things I suggest you do to help you receive revelation concerning God's love for you:

- Tell yourself, in your mind and out loud, "God loves me." Say it, and let it sink in. Repeat it often: when you awake in the morning, when you go to bed at night, and throughout the entire day. Look at yourself in the mirror, point to yourself, call yourself by name, and say, "_______, God loves you."
- Keep a diary, a book of remembrance, of special things that God does for you. Include little things as well as major things. Read over your list at least once a week, and you will be encouraged. Let this become a Holy Ghost project. I think you will have fun with it, as I did.
- Learn, and even commit to memory, several scriptures about the love of God for you.
- Read some good books about God's love. I recommend that you start with the ones I have written called *Tell Them I Love Them*, and *Reduce Me to Love*.[5]
- Pray for the Holy Spirit, Who is the Teacher, to give you a revelation of God's love.

6

Follow the Holy Spirit

IF YOU ARRIVE at the conclusion that you need emotional healing, and that many of the problems you face are a result of bad roots from the past, you may become anxious to get rid of those roots of the problem so you can be made well. That is understandable, but it is important to allow the Holy Spirit to lead, guide, and direct you in that healing process.

God has already sent Jesus Christ to come to earth and purchase your complete healing. Once that was accomplished, He sent His Holy Spirit to administer to you what Jesus bought by His blood.

Jesus told His disciples that it was better for them that He go away to be with the Father, because if He did not go, the Comforter could not come (see John 16:7). The Comforter is the Holy Spirit. In *The Amplified Bible* version of this verse Jesus calls the Holy Spirit our Counselor, Helper, Advocate, Intercessor, Strengthener, and Standby. During your recovery process, you will need to experience every facet of the Holy Spirit's ministry.

SEEK ONLY GODLY COUNSEL

Don't run around seeking counsel from just anyone. Pray first, asking the Lord whether it is His will that you go to another human being for counsel, or whether He desires to counsel you Himself.

In my own life I have had many, many problems, yet I never went to anyone else for counsel with the exception of one time. On this occasion I visited a lady in ministry who had been abused herself. I do not mean to discredit her, but she really was not able to help me. It was not her fault; she simply was not anointed by the Lord to do so.

God is not obligated to anoint what He does not initiate. So often people run to others without following the guidance and leadership of the Holy Spirit, and it never bears good, lasting fruit. *When you are in trouble, go to the throne before you go to the phone.*

I do not mean to suggest that it is wrong to seek counsel. I am just suggesting that you pray and allow the Lord to lead and guide you through the Holy Spirit. Let Him choose the right counselor for you. Just because a person has been through what you are going through, or is a close personal friend, does not mean that individual is the right counselor for you. So I repeat, pray!

I am definitely not saying that you should not seek counsel just because I didn't. We all have different personalities. I happen to have a strong, determined, self-disciplined, goal-oriented personality. These traits helped me to keep moving toward my objective, which was emotional wholeness. Others may need someone to help them along a bit, someone to assist them in setting goals for themselves and to keep striving toward those goals.

It is vital to follow the leading of the Holy Spirit. He is the best Counselor. Either He will help you directly, or He will guide you to someone through whom He can minister to you. In either case, you should ultimately look to Him for your help. Even the counsel that other people may offer you will not become *rhema* (a personal revelation from God) to you without the help of the Holy Spirit.

It is also important to realize that God has different calls on our lives. Since He has called me to teach His Word, it was better for me to receive the truth I needed directly from Him. However, that is not a rule for everyone.

The Ministry of the Holy Spirit

Another reason the ministry of the Holy Spirit is so important is found in John 16:8 in which Jesus says that it is the Holy Spirit Who *convicts and convinces* of sin and of righteousness.

Most people who have been abused are shame-based individuals. (The topic of shame will be discussed in detail in a later chapter.) They feel bad about themselves. They do not like themselves; therefore, they experience a lot of guilt and condemnation.

It is the devil who brings condemnation; the Holy Spirit brings conviction. (There is a difference. I welcome conviction, but I resist condemnation—and so should you.) Only the Holy Spirit, through the Word of God and His power to change, can convince a shame-based person that he has been made righteous through the shed blood of Jesus Christ: "For our sake He made Christ [virtually] to be sin Who knew no sin, so that in *and* through Him we might become [endued with, viewed as being in, and examples of] the righteousness of God [what we ought to be, approved and acceptable and in right relationship with Him, by His goodness]" (2 Corinthians 5:21).

Jesus referred to the Holy Spirit as the Spirit of Truth and assured us that He will guide us into all the Truth—the whole, full Truth (see John 16:13). Jesus also said that the Holy Spirit will prompt our memory: "But the Comforter (Counselor, Helper, Intercessor, Advocate, Strengthener, Standby), the Holy Spirit, Whom the Father will send in My name [in My place, to represent Me and act on My behalf], He will teach you all things. And He will cause you to recall (will remind you of, bring to your remembrance) everything I have told you" (John 14:26). Both of these aspects of the ministry of the Spirit are major areas of assistance for those who are in recovery from abuse. Such people must get out of their denial and face the truth. There may be things they have forgotten because they are too painful to remember, things that will have to be recalled and faced during the healing process.

If the person in charge of the recovery is not led by the Spirit, he sometimes can take the abused person through the process too quickly. If too accelerated, it can become more painful than the person can handle.

I remember a girl who once came to me in a prayer line. She was very upset and extremely emotional, almost panic-stricken. She began to relate to me that every week when she went to visit her counselor, it was so painful that it was almost more than she could bear. In her anxiety, I heard her say several times, "It is just too much; it hurts so bad, I cannot stand it."

At the time she was speaking, I was praying and asking the Lord to help me so I could help her. I was actually concerned that she might become hysterical right there at the altar. Suddenly I received an answer from the Lord. I felt that probably her counselor was not sensitive to the Spirit and that she was having this young woman face issues so fast that her mind and her emotional system were unable to handle it all.

When I said to the girl, "Listen to me, I think I know what the problem is," she quieted down long enough for me to share what God was saying. As she listened, she immediately began to get some relief. She agreed that what I was describing was exactly what was happening.

I shared with her that during my own healing process, the Holy Spirit led me to many different resources for guidance. The first was a book that my husband suggested I read. It was the testimony of a woman who had been abused as a child. Until that time, I did not think that any of my problems were a result of my past.

That book was so difficult for me to read. When I came to the part in which the woman began describing in detail how her stepfather had sexually abused her, the memories, pain, anger, and rage began rushing up in me from somewhere deep inside. I threw that book on the floor and loudly exclaimed, "I will not read this!"

Just then I heard the Holy Spirit reply, "It is time."

I had been attempting to walk with God for several years when this event took place. Why hadn't He led me to something that could have helped me sooner? The answer is because it was not time! The Holy Spirit knows precisely the right timing in our lives. I always say, "Only the Spirit knows when you are ready for what." In other words, the Spirit of the Lord is the only One Who knows what it will take to help you, and when you are ready to receive that help.

It may come in the form of a book, a certain speaker, or a friend who says just what you need to hear at the moment. Or it may come through a personal testimony, or even a direct dealing from the Lord Himself. Today may be God's appointed time for you as you are reading this book. If so, God will use it in some area in which you are hurting at the present. It may be the beginning of your recovery, the next step in that process, or even the finishing touch in your long struggle for wholeness.

Many people who come to me for prayer for emotional healing are concerned and even distraught because there are portions of their childhood that they cannot recall. They have been on what I call "digging expeditions," trying to unearth forgotten memories so they can face them, deal with them, and get them out of their system. I tell such people that there are still portions of my own past that I cannot recall. Actually, much of my childhood seems to be filled with blank pages.

I remind people that the Holy Spirit leads us into all truth and is able to bring many things to our remembrance. But we must allow Him to do the leading in this sensitive area. I have put Him in charge of my memory. I truly believe that if remembering something from my past is going to help me, then I will recall it. If it will not help me, is unnecessary, or would even be harmful for me to remember, then I am thankful that I cannot recall it. I believe that sometimes what we do not know cannot hurt us.

Obviously, this is not always the case. Many times people experience great relief by recalling some traumatic event, dealing with it, and then getting on with their lives. Sometimes, if memories have been shut out on purpose and suppressed deep within the recesses of the mind, they will poison the entire system. In that case, the memories must be exposed before wholeness can be established. Yet, here again, it is important to remember that if this process is not done with the leadership and guidance of the Holy Spirit, it can be harmful and actually cause even more damage to already wounded emotions.

The Holy Spirit is gentle, tender, considerate, kind, loving, and patient. Yet, He is also powerful and mighty and able to do what people can never do on their own. The psalmist says, "EXCEPT THE Lord builds the house, they labor in vain who build it; except the Lord keeps the city, the watchman wakes but in vain" (Psalm 127:1). I spent many years of my life waking and laboring in vain. I encourage you not to waste the most precious years of your life trying to "do it yourself." Seek God and His plan for your recovery. He will lead you one step at a time, and you will be transformed "from glory to glory" (see 2 Corinthians 3:18 KJV).

7

The Two Kinds of Pain

EVEN WHEN WE allow the Holy Spirit to lead us, emotional healing is still painful. But I believe there are two kinds of pain: the pain of change, and the pain of never changing and remaining the same. If you will let the Spirit of the Lord direct your recovery program, He will always be there to provide the strength you need in each phase, so that whatever trials you may have to face, you will be able to bear them.

The Lord has promised never to leave us nor forsake us. This promise in Hebrews 13:5 is so powerful: "Let your character *or* moral disposition be free from love of money [including greed, avarice, lust, and craving for earthly possessions] and be satisfied with your present [circumstances and with what you have]; for He [God] Himself has said, I will not in any way fail you *nor* give you up *nor* leave you without support. [I will] not, [I will] not, [I will] not in any degree leave you helpless *nor* forsake *nor* let [you] down (relax My hold on you)! [Assuredly not!]"

We need to hold on to that promise when we are tempted to get ahead of God. If we begin to "do our own thing," we are in dangerous territory. Our heavenly Father is under no obligation to sustain us in bearing trials that were never a part of His plan for us. We may well survive, but the process will involve much more struggle than was necessary.

The pain of emotional wounding and healing can be even more traumatic than physical pain. When you are following God's revealed plan, and you come to painful times, remember that the Holy Spirit is the Strengthener. Sometimes it may seem that you are not going to make it through. At such moments, ask the Lord to strengthen you.

A great scripture to memorize for these difficult times is 1 Corinthians 10:13 in which the apostle Paul reminds us:

> For no temptation (no trial regarded as enticing to sin, no matter how it comes or where it leads) has overtaken you *and* laid hold on you that is not common to man [that is, no temptation or trial has come to you that is beyond human resistance and that is not adjusted and adapted and belonging to human experience, and such as man can bear]. But God is faithful [to His Word and to His compassionate nature], and He [can be trusted] not to let you be tempted *and* tried *and* assayed beyond your ability *and* strength of resistance *and* power to endure, but with the temptation He will [always] also provide the way out (the means of escape to a landing place), that you may be capable *and* strong *and* powerful to bear up under it patiently.

With such hard times come many temptations. Among these is the temptation to give up and revert to old thoughts and ways, to become negative, depressed, and angry with God because you do not understand why He does not seem to be providing the way out of all the pain you have had to bear in your life. Yet this passage of Scripture tells us that God will always intervene on our behalf and that His help will always arrive on time. Purpose in your heart to hold on and not let go!

Another helpful passage is found in 2 Corinthians 12:7-9 in which Paul refers to his own suffering because of what he calls "a thorn (a splinter) in the flesh" (v. 7). It really does not matter what the thorn was, but we know it irritated him and he wanted it removed. Whatever it was, three times Paul sought God to take it away. Yet the Lord's answer to him was, "My grace (My favor and loving-kindness and mercy) is enough for you [sufficient against any danger and enables you to bear the trouble manfully]; for *My* strength *and* power are made perfect (fulfilled and completed) *and show themselves most effective* in [your] weakness" (v. 9).

We are not always delivered from our distress at the precise moment we call on the name of the Lord. Sometimes we must endure for a while, be patient, and continue in faith. Thank God, during those times in which the Lord decides for whatever reason not to deliver us right away, He always gives us the grace and strength we need to press on toward eventual victory.

Do you ever wonder why God does not always deliver us from our bondage and problems immediately? The reason is because only the Lord knows everything that needs to be done in the lives of His children—and the perfect timing for it to be done.

From my own experience, I have learned to trust rather than to question. It is not wrong to ask God why, unless that questioning produces confusion, in which case it is much better simply to trust the Lord, knowing that He is never wrong—and that He is never late! Often we understand the why behind an event or situation only after it is all over and we can stand on the other side of it, looking back on it. There are many experiences in my life that I certainly did not understand while I was going through them. Now, however, I have come to understand something of their meaning and purpose.

Going through trials is painful. In my ministry, I often share with people that the book of Revelation says that we overcome the devil by the blood of the Lamb and by the word of our testimony (see Revelation 12:11 KJV). A testimony of victory in any area of life is important. However, in order to have a positive testimony, it is necessary to have successfully overcome some hardship or opposition.

The painful part is what we must go through while we are being tempted and tested; the glorious part comes after we have finished going through the trial and can then testify of the great victory and God's great faithfulness. *We have no testimony without a test.*

Doorways of Pain

Because I personally experienced so much emotional pain, as you may have done also, I grew weary of hurting. I was attempting to find healing by following the leadership of the Holy Spirit. Yet I could not honestly understand why the process had to be so painful. I felt that if I were to be able to continue enduring the pain, I had to have some answers from the Lord. I was actually improving, getting better, gaining a victory here and there, but it seemed that every time I made any progress, the Lord would bring me into a new phase of recovery that would always mean more pain and emotional upset.

As I prayed about my situation, God gave me a vision. In my heart, I saw a series of doorways—one after another. Each represented a traumatic event in my past life that had brought pain when it had occurred. The Lord showed me how that each time I went though one of the painful events or situa-

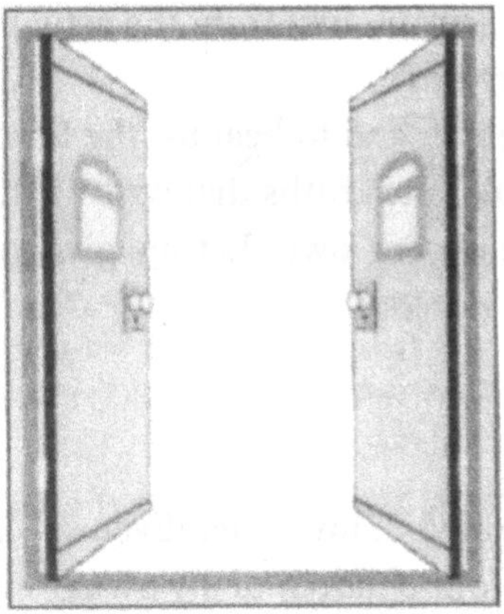

The Doorways of Pain

tions (being sexually abused at home; being ridiculed at school because I was overweight; being unable to have any close friends; being subjected to constant fear; being abandoned by my first husband; being betrayed by a group of friends at church; and so on), it was a new doorway of pain, through which I was forced to pass.

I can remember vividly the anguish of fear, rejection, abandonment, and betrayal—and so can you if you were a victim of these abuses that place people into such bondage.

When I finally allowed the Lord to work in my life, He revealed to me I had been hiding behind many such "doorways of pain." I was deep in bondage, taking refuge behind false personalities, pretenses, and facades. I was simply unable to understand how to free myself. When the Lord began to deliver me from bondage, it hurt.

I now understand that in order to be led out of bondage and into freedom, we must pass back through the same, or similar, doorways of pain that we previously went through so that we can get on the other side of them. When we are taken into bondage through doorways of pain, we must pass through the same doorways to get out of its captivity. Both times through the doorways is painful, first from the actual abuse, and again from the memory of it.

In order to deliver and to heal us, the Lord must lead us to face issues, people, and truths that we find difficult, if not impossible, to face on our own. Let me give you several examples:

Example One

I was always terrified of my father. Even as a grown woman in my forties, with four children of my own, I was still frightened of him. Many painful events had brought that fear into my life.

I was forty-seven years old before the Lord led me to finally confront my father. I will share more about this confrontation later in this book, but I had to look my father straight in the eye and tell him, "I am not afraid of you anymore."

When I finally spoke to my father about the abusive way he had treated me, I did it in obedience and by faith, but not without "fear and trembling" (see Philippians 2:12 KJV). I had come face to face with one of my doorways of pain. I knew that either I could go back through it and come out free on the other side, or I could stay in bondage behind the door, hiding, and remain forever afraid of my own father.

It is important to note that *I confronted my father, who was the primary cause of my pain, only because the Holy Spirit led me to do so. Do not confront your abuser just because I did it.* You must pray and listen to God's leading concerning the right steps to your deliverance.

Example Two

Sometimes people get hurt in the church by other Christians. Somehow we seem to think that believers should not hurt other believers—and they shouldn't. But things are seldom as they ought to be, even in the lives of God's people. We in the Church do hurt one another, and it does cause pain.

Frequently, when this happens, the injured party withdraws from any association or involvement with the ones who caused the pain. Hiding behind a doorway of pain, the wounded individual may decide: "Since I got hurt at church, I will continue to go to services (maybe), but I will never get involved with those people again." That is a form of bondage, because the person is allowing the past to control him.

God will bring us to a place in which we must step out of hiding and take a chance on being hurt again. When we do step out, it is the equivalent of going back through the same doorway of pain that led us into bondage.

Example Three

Learning to submit to authority can be difficult for some people. It was extremely painful for me. Since I had been abused by every authority figure I had ever known, my attitude was, "Why should I allow someone else to tell me what to do?" I did not trust anyone, especially men.

When the Holy Spirit led me to the phase of my recovery in which I had to submit to my husband, the battle was on! I experienced a terrible sense of rebellion in my flesh. I wanted to be submissive, because I truly believed that it was scriptural, but the pain of submission was more then I knew how to handle.

I did not understand what was wrong with me. I realize now that submitting to someone else and allowing that person to make decisions for me brought back all the old fears and memories of being manipulated and taken advantage of. Having my father (an authority figure) telling me that the hurtful decisions he was making for me were for *my* good, and all the time hating so much what he was doing to me, combined with my frustrations at being unable to do anything about it all, did not leave me thrilled about submission.

In order to be set free and to become the whole person that God desired for me to be, I had to learn to submit to my husband. Like many other Christians, I believed that the Scriptures teach that submission of the wife and children to the husband and father as the head of the home is God's revealed plan for families. I was convinced that this principle is set forth in His Word and that therefore I had no choice but to submit to it, or be in rebellion against the Lord. But it certainly was painful! Now, I am free and can see the safety and security in godly submission.

Many people get confused about submission. They think that it means that they must do everything an authority tells them to do, no matter what it is. The Bible teaches that we should be submissive only "as it is fit in the Lord" (Colossians 3:18 KJV).

I trust that these examples will help you understand the "doorways of pain" and how they must be faced. Do not look upon them as the entrance to suffering but as the threshold of recovery. Jesus will always be with you to lead you and strengthen you as you pass through these gateways to wholeness.

Remember, *pain is really a part of the healing process*. If a person falls on concrete and skins his knee badly, he will most definitely hurt. The next day, the pain may be even worse than when the wound was fresh. By that time a scab may have formed over the wound, which is a sign that his body is involved in the process of healing. But although now covered with the protective scab, his wound is also drawing, burning, and throbbing because of the increase of blood rushing to bring healing to the affected area.

The initial wound brings pain, but often healing brings even worse pain. Yet they are not the same kind of pain, nor do they have the same result. Some people's emotional wounds have been ignored for so long they have become infected. That kind of pain is totally different from the pain of healing. One is to be avoided; the other is to be welcomed.

No Pain, No Gain!

I gained an excellent piece of wisdom through personal experience: Do not be afraid of pain! As strange as it may seem, the more you dread and resist the pain of healing, the more you increase the effect that pain has upon you.

An example of this truth happened years ago when I went on a fast for the first time in my life. God called me to a twenty-eight-day juice fast. In the beginning, I went through some really hard times. I was very, very hungry. In fact, I was so famished that I was in actual pain. As I cried out to the Lord, complaining that I just could not stand it any longer, He answered me. Deep within me I heard the "still small voice" (see 1 Kings 19:12 KJV) of the Lord say to me, "Stop fighting the pain; let it do its work." From that time on, the fast was much easier, even enjoyable, because I knew that every time I felt discomfort, it was a sign of progress.

The rule is that the more pain is resisted, the stronger it becomes. When a pregnant woman goes into labor, the advice she is given by her attendants is, "Relax." They know that the more she fights the pain, the stronger it will become, and the longer the delivery process will take.

When you are going through a difficult time, when the pain becomes so severe that it seems to be more than you can endure, remember Hebrews 12:2: "Looking away [from all that will distract] to Jesus, Who is the Leader *and* the Source of our faith [giving the first incentive for our belief] and is also its Finisher [bringing it to maturity and perfection]. He, for the joy [of obtaining the prize] that was set before Him, endured the cross, despising *and* ignoring the shame, and is now seated at the right hand of the throne of God."

Endurance Produces Joy

When you are experiencing pain, do not fight it. Allow it to accomplish its purpose. Remember this promise: "They who sow in tears shall reap in joy *and* singing" (Psalm 126:5). *Learn to endure whatever you need to, knowing that there is joy on the other side!*

Healing may be painful, but you have nothing to lose. You are hurting anyway; you may as well reap the full benefit of your suffering. As long as you allow past abuse to keep you in bondage, you will live in continual pain. At least the pain of healing produces a positive result—joy, instead of misery.

Let your pain lead you out of bondage, not deeper into it. Do the right thing, even if it is hard. Obey God and follow the leading of the Holy Spirit, knowing that "weeping may endure for a night, but joy comes in the morning" (Psalm 30:5).

8

The Only Way Out Is Through

IN ONE OF our meetings, a woman came forward asking us to pray for a certain bondage to be broken in her life. As soon as I started to pray for her, she began to cry. Almost immediately I received a vision of her standing on a track, as though she were about to run a race. As I watched, I saw that every time the race would begin, and she would start moving toward the finish line, she would go about halfway and then turn around and come back to the starting line.

After a while, she would repeat the process. This happened time after time. I shared with her what I was seeing and told her that I believed that God was saying to her, "This time, you need to go all the way through." As I shared that message with her, she immediately agreed that God was speaking to her. Her problem was that although she often made some progress toward emotional healing, she always gave up under pressure.

Now she was determined to see the process through to complete victory.

It is always much harder to finish than it is to start. There really are no "quick-fix" methods to emotional healing. In 2 Corinthians 3:18 the apostle Paul speaks of Christians being transformed "from one degree of glory to another." If you are going through the difficult process of emotional healing, I encourage you to enjoy the degree of "glory" you are currently experiencing as you move toward the next level.

Many people turn emotional healing or recovery from abuse into such an ordeal that they never allow themselves to enjoy any aspect of it. Do not allow yourself to be tempted to focus on how far you have to go. Instead look at how far you have come!

Remember that *you have a life to live while you are being healed!* Adopt this as your attitude: I am not where I need to be, but, thank God, I am not where I used to be. I'm okay, and I'm on my way!

Going Through

In some aspects, spiritual growth can be compared to physical growth. There are certain stages that we have to go through in order to mature. I think it would be safe to say that many people do not enjoy their children while they are raising them. At each stage of growth, the parents wish the child were in another stage. If the child is crawling, they wish he were walking, out of diapers, in school, graduating, getting married, giving them grandchildren, and on and on.

We should learn to enjoy each stage of life as it comes because each has joys and trials uniquely its own. As Christians, we are growing throughout our lifetime. We never stop progressing. Make a decision right now to begin to enjoy yourself while you are striving to reach each new level of victory.

In Deuteronomy 7:22, Moses told the children of Israel that the Lord would drive out their enemies before them "little by little." Between each victory in our lives, there is a time of waiting. During this time the Holy Spirit deals with us, opening to us new revelations, helping us to face and receive even greater truths. The waiting is usually difficult for most of us because impatience is always present within us to stir up dissatisfaction. We want everything now!

PATIENCE REAPS PROMISES

A lot of people want blessings, but they do not want to prepare for them. John the Baptist came out of the wilderness crying, "Prepare ye the way of the Lord" (Matthew 3:3 KJV). He wanted people to know that Jesus was coming to do a work in their lives, but they needed to be prepared.

The Bible says, "Eye has not seen and ear has not heard and has not entered into the heart of man, [all that] God has prepared (made and keeps ready) for those who love Him [who hold Him in affectionate reverence, promptly obeying Him and gratefully recognizing the benefits He has bestowed]" (1 Corinthians 2:9).

It requires spiritual maturity to walk through difficulties in faith that God has something good planned for us. But we need to understand that going through is usually the only way out. We need faith, patience, and endurance in order to receive the end result of all that God promises we are to receive. This passage from Hebrews explains:

> Do not, therefore, fling away your fearless confidence, for it carries a great *and* glorious compensation of reward.

> For you have need of steadfast patience *and* endurance, so that you may perform *and* fully accomplish the will of God, and thus receive *and* carry away [and enjoy to the full] what is promised.
>
> For still a little while (a very little while), and the Coming One will come and He will not delay. (Hebrews 10:35-37)

In Hebrews 6:11 we read: "But we do [strongly and earnestly] desire for each of you to show the same diligence *and* sincerity [all the way through] in realizing *and* enjoying the full assurance *and* development of [your] hope until the end."

In Isaiah 43:1-2, the Lord admonishes His people, saying:

> Fear not, for I have redeemed you [ransomed you by paying a price instead of leaving you captives]; I have called you by your name; you are Mine.
>
> When you pass *through* the waters, I will be with you, and *through* the rivers, they will not overwhelm you. When you walk *through* the fire, you will not be burned *or* scorched, nor will the flame kindle upon you. (Emphasis mine)

David said of the Lord, "Though I walk through the [deep, sunless] valley of the shadow of death, I will fear *or* dread no evil, for You are with me; Your rod [to protect] and Your staff [to guide], they comfort me" (Psalm 23:4).

Often a person who is rooted in abuse ends up with strongholds in his mind and flesh that must be allowed to pass through the valley of the shadow of death if those strongholds are ever to be pulled down and destroyed.

Paul explains that we war against the enemy by capturing our thoughts that do not line up with what Christ said, and bringing them into subjection to what the Word says to do and believe:

> For though we walk (live) in the flesh, we are not carrying on our warfare according to the flesh *and* using mere human weapons.
>
> For the weapons of our warfare are not physical [weapons of flesh and blood], but they are mighty before God for the overthrow *and* destruction of strongholds,
>
> [Inasmuch as we] refute arguments *and* theories *and* reasonings and every proud *and* lofty thing that sets itself up against the [true] knowledge of God; and we lead every thought *and* purpose away captive into the obedience of Christ (the Messiah, the Anointed One). (2 Corinthians 10:3-5)

For example, as a result of having been abused for so long, I developed an independent personality. I did not trust anyone. Early in life I came to the conclusion that if I took care of myself and never asked anyone for anything, then I would get hurt less. As the Lord began to reveal to me that my independent attitude was not scriptural, I had to "walk through the valley of the shadow of death." In other words, I had to let that old nature (part of the old Joyce) go to the cross and die.

The temptation is to run away from our problems, but the Lord says that we are to go through them. The good news is that He has promised that we will never have to go through them alone. He will always be there to help us in every way. He has said to us, "Fear not, for I am with you."

It is in going through things with the Lord that our faith is built up in Him. I love the story of Shadrach, Meshach, and Abednego found in Daniel, chapter 3. The king had warned them to bow down and worship him or he would throw them into a fiery furnace.

They said, "Well, if God can deliver us, He will, but even if He does not deliver us, we will not bow and worship you." They knew that God was capable of delivering them, but if that was not His plan, they were still going to keep their integrity before the Lord and not give up serving Him. We all need to commit to serving God with that determination.

So the three men were thrown into the furnace, and the king turned up the heat seven times hotter than it was before. This reminds me of those times when we make the right decision, but it seems that our troubles multiply.

I like this story, because it says that Shadrach, Meshach, and Abednego were bound and thrown into the fire, but that when the king looked into the fire, they were loosed. Sometimes we go into problems all bound, but it is in the problem, going through things, that we get loosed and delivered. The king saw a fourth man in the fire with them—remember Jesus said, "Fear not, for I am with you."

When Shadrach, Meshach, and Abednego were brought out, they did not even smell like smoke. I relate to these men, because the devil tried to destroy me. I went through so much pain from the abuse in my life, and when I tried to get free from it I found more pain that I could not understand. Then God showed me how we go through things that put us in bondage, but we have to go through the same things to get back out.

When we begin our journey to wholeness with the Lord, we are usually all knotted up inside with fear. Fear is the enemy of confidence. People can be afraid of many things, of driving cars, of being alone, and of some deep-seated phobias.

I think of F.E.A.R. as False Evidence Appearing Real. If the devil can frighten us, then we are putting more faith in what he says than in what God says. It is one thing to feel fear, but fear will control us if we do not stand our ground and face our fears.

A woman was sharing how fear was keeping her from doing things that she needed to do. So her friend said, "Well, do it afraid." That was life-changing advice for me. Sometimes we have to face our fears and just "do it afraid."

As we allow God to do so, He begins to straighten up our lives by untying "one knot of fear at a time." He helps us go through hard things and discover that His promises are true. We cannot spend our lives running away from everything we fear.

Some people are so afraid of elevators they will turn down a job that is located on an upper floor of a building. If they want the job, they need to get on that elevator, pray, go up a few floors, get off, breathe, and repeat the process until they overcome their fear. We need to overcome our fears that keep us from carrying out God's perfect will for our lives.

The Bible is full of scriptures that say, "Fear not," because God knew that Satan was going to try to use fear to keep His people from fulfilling their destiny in Him.

To some of His first disciples Jesus said, "I am the Way, follow Me." When you decide to follow Jesus, you will soon learn that He never turns back in fear. His path is always straightforward to the finish line. Do not be like the woman in my prayer line who always gave up halfway through the race. As difficult as it may be, decide to stay in the race and see it through!

9

Let Go of the Past

I ENCOURAGE PEOPLE to let go of their past, but never to run from it. The only way to gain victory over the pain of our past is to let God walk us back through that doorway of pain and into victory. No one can achieve victory for us; we have to work out our own salvation. Paul explained this truth in his letter to the Philippian church, saying:

> Therefore, my dear ones . . . work out (cultivate, carry out to the goal, and fully complete) your own salvation with reverence *and* awe and trembling (self-distrust, with serious caution, tenderness of conscience, watchfulness against temptation, timidly shrinking from whatever might offend God and discredit the name of Christ).
>
> [Not in your own strength] for it is God Who is all the while effectually at work in you [energizing and creating in you the power and desire], both to will and to work for His good pleasure *and* satisfaction *and* delight. (Philippians 2:12, 13)

We have to let God take us through things, and let Him work in us so our mess becomes our message. Difficult things that we have endured in our past prepare us for God's blessings in our future.

Even Jesus had a time of training for His future. Hebrews 5:8-9 says, "Although He was a Son, He learned [active, special] obedience through what He suffered and, [His completed experience] making Him perfectly [equipped], He became the Author *and* Source of eternal salvation to all those who give heed *and* obey Him."

There was a period in the life of Jesus in which we are told nothing about what was happening to Him. During this time we know that He was *growing*. We too have times of growth that we may not be able to talk about to anyone. It is an intimate time of growth that we must endure. There may be things going on inside of us that we do not understand. But when we finally arrive at the place God wants to bring us, we will see how our past prepared us for what God wanted for us all along.

I like the story about the couple who went into an antique shop one day and found a beautiful teacup sitting on a shelf. They took it off the shelf, so they could look at it more closely, and said, "We really want to buy this gorgeous cup."

All of the sudden, the teacup began to talk, saying, "I wasn't always like this. There was a time when I was just a cold, hard, colorless lump of clay. One day my master picked me up and said, 'I could do something with this.' Then he started to pat me, and roll me, and change my shape.

"I said, 'What are you doing? That hurts. I don't know if I want to look like this! Stop!' But he said, 'Not yet.'

"Then he put me on a wheel and began to spin me around and around and around, until I screamed, 'Let me off, I am getting dizzy!' 'Not yet,' he said.

"Then he shaped me into a cup and put me in a hot oven. I

cried, 'Let me out! It's hot in here, I am suffocating.' But he just looked at me through that little glass window and smiled and said, 'Not yet.'

"When he took me out, I thought his work on me was over, but then he started to paint me. I couldn't believe what he did next. He put me back into the oven, and I said, 'You have to believe me, I can't stand this! Please let me out!' But he said, 'Not yet.'

"Finally, he took me out of the oven and set me up on a shelf where I thought he had forgotten me. Then one day he took me off the shelf and held me before a mirror. I couldn't believe my eyes, I had become a beautiful teacup that everyone wants to buy."

Submit to the Potter's Hands

God has an awesome plan for our lives, and sometimes He starts changing things so fast that we feel dizzy and disoriented, like a lump of clay on a potter's wheel. But we have to trust that He is working out what is best for us (see Romans 8:28). We need to just go with the flow and let Him make us into something beautiful. Isaiah understood this process when he wrote, "You have hidden Your face from us . . . Yet, O Lord, You are our Father; we are the clay, and You our Potter, and we all are the work of Your hand" (Isaiah 64:7-8).

To live a victorious Christian life, we have to be willing to let go of the past, die to self, forgive those who have hurt us, and let God take us on to the place of promised blessings that He has prepared for us. No one can promise that everything we want to be different in our lives will be changed into what we want it to be. Some things may never change the way we want them to, but God can change *us* so much that we will not care.

Our comfort has to be in Christ. We need to forget about what others think about us, or what people have done to us in the past. We are to keep our attention on what God wants to do in us, and with us, and for us now. Paul wrote, "For in Him we live and move and have our being" (Acts 17:28).

Letting go of the past involves looking to the future in a new way. In Galatians 2:20, Paul offers us a promise that we, who need to let go of past hurts, can now confess: "I have been crucified with Christ [in Him I have shared His crucifixion]; it is no longer I who live, but Christ (the Messiah) lives in me; and the life I now live in the body I live by faith in (by adherence to and reliance on and complete trust in) the Son of God, Who loved me and gave Himself up for me."

We need to learn to be satisfied by being in God's will. The more we focus on who we are in Christ, the less it matters who we were in the past, or even what has happened to us. Paul said, "I count everything as loss compared to the possession of the priceless privilege (the overwhelming preciousness, the surpassing worth, and supreme advantage) of knowing Christ Jesus my Lord *and* of progressively becoming more deeply *and* intimately acquainted with Him [of perceiving and recognizing and understanding Him more fully and clearly]" (Philippians 3:8).

He added, "[For my determined purpose is] that I may know Him [that I may progressively become more deeply and intimately acquainted with Him, perceiving and recognizing and understanding the wonders of His Person more strongly and more clearly], and that I may in that same way come to know the power outflowing from His resurrection [which it exerts over believers], and that I may so share His sufferings as to be continually transformed [in spirit into His likeness even] to His death, [in the hope] that if possible I may attain to the [spiritual and moral] resurrection [that lifts me] out from among the dead [even while in the body]" (Philippians 3:10-11).

There are deep places to discover in God, and there are deep places in us that only God can fill. We need to understand the power of God's resurrection, power that can lift us out from among the dead even while we live in the body. Just as the eagle rests its wings on the currents of the air to lift itself above the clouds, Christ will lift us above the storms of our lives.

We may have a goal to move toward perfection, but we will never arrive at that state until Jesus comes again. We are to accept ourselves, love ourselves, and enjoy the journey because we know God is working on our future all of the time.

Press On to What Lies Ahead

Paul went on to write:

> Not that I have now attained [this ideal], or have already been made perfect, but I press on to lay hold of (grasp) *and* make my own, that for which Christ Jesus (the Messiah) has laid hold of me *and* made me His own. I do not consider, brethren, that I have captured *and* made it my own [yet]; but one thing I do [it is my one aspiration]: *forgetting what lies behind and straining forward to what lies ahead, I press on* toward the goal to win the [supreme and heavenly] prize to which God in Christ Jesus is calling us upward" (Philippians 3:12-14, emphasis mine).

If you have been miserable because of the things that have happened in your past, I encourage you to do as I did and set your focus in a new direction. Determine to be what God wants you to be, to have what God wants you to have, and to receive what Jesus died to give you.

When you are ready for change, say, "I am not going to live in bondage anymore. I am not going to live in a box, comparing myself to others, and trying to be what they say I should be. I cannot do anything about what I have done in the past, but I can do something about my future. I am going to enjoy my life and have what Jesus died for me to have. I am going to let go of the past, and go on pursuing God from this day forth."

It takes maturity to let go of the past, but a mature Christian receives the fullness of God's blessings. You can forget old failures, old disappointments, and old relationships that did not work out. Instead, you can discover the new mercies that God is ready to give you every day because of the covenant He made with you when you put your trust in His Son Jesus Christ to save you.

King David searched for relatives of his predecessor King Saul because he wanted to bless them, simply because he had a covenant relationship with Saul's son Jonathan. In 2 Samuel 9 is the story of how David found Jonathan's crippled son, Mephibosheth, and brought him into the royal palace where he could take care of him. Mephibosheth did not *do* anything to deserve this protection and provision, except that he had a relationship to one who had a covenant with David.

This is a picture of why God cares for us. He blesses us because, as believers, we have a relationship with His Son. We do not deserve to be blessed. We do not earn blessings. We may even be crippled emotionally from some incident in our past. But God picks us up and restores us to our rightful place in His kingdom of peace.

God is not waiting for us to do all the right things before He blesses us. In fact, the most anointed prayer we can ever pray is, "Lord, help me." We cannot reach perfection apart from

God. We must be totally dependent on Him to keep His promises in our lives. We are only called to be "believers"; otherwise, we would be called "achievers."

The disciples asked Jesus, "What are we to do, that we may [habitually] be working the works of God? [What are we to do to carry out what God requires?]" (John 6:28).

Jesus replied, "This is the work (service) that God asks of you: that *you believe in the One Whom He has sent* [that you cleave to, trust, rely on, and have faith in His Messenger]" (v. 29).

Verses 1-12 of Psalm 51 offers a powerful prayer for us to pray:

> HAVE MERCY upon me, O God, according to Your steadfast love; according to the multitude of Your tender mercy *and* loving-kindness blot out my transgressions.
>
> Wash me thoroughly [and repeatedly] from my iniquity *and* guilt and cleanse me *and* make me wholly pure from my sin!
>
> For I am conscious of my transgressions *and* I acknowledge them; my sin is ever before me.
>
> Against You, You only, have I sinned and done that which is evil in Your sight, so that You are justified in Your sentence and faultless in Your judgment.
>
> Behold, I was brought forth in [a state of] iniquity; my mother was sinful who conceived me [and I too am sinful].
>
> Behold, You desire truth in the inner being; make me therefore to know wisdom in my inmost heart.
>
> Purify me with hyssop, and I shall be clean [ceremonially]; wash me, and I shall [in reality] be whiter than snow.
>
> Make me to hear joy and gladness *and* be satisfied; let the bones which You have broken rejoice.
>
> Hide Your face from my sins and blot out all my guilt *and* iniquities.

> Create in me a clean heart, O God, and renew a right, persevering, *and* steadfast spirit within me.
>
> Cast me not away from Your presence and take not Your Holy Spirit from me.
>
> Restore to me the joy of Your salvation and uphold me with a willing spirit.

If we simply ask God, He will deliver us from the pain of our past mistakes and create in us a steadfast spirit. But while we do not have to *do* anything to receive God's deliverance, we can miss out on blessings if we run away from our problems without letting God bring us through them.

Moses looked for the easy way out of his problems after he had stepped out of God's timing. He had killed an Egyptian, and there had been a witness to the murder, so he ran into the wilderness to hide. Before God called Moses to go forward to the promised land, He told Moses to *go back* to Egypt (see Exodus 3:1-10), saying, "Because I have most assuredly seen the abuse *and* oppression of My people in Egypt and have heard their sighing *and* groaning, I have come down to rescue them. So, now come! I will send you back to Egypt [as My messenger]" (Acts 7:34).

God was sending Moses back to the people who had "denied (disowned and rejected)" him (Acts 7:35). His own people had mocked him, saying, "Who made you our ruler (referee) and judge?" (see Exodus 2:14). Moses probably was not excited about going back to face his problems in Egypt.

God does not always call us to go back physically to a place we have been. But if, for example, we have a difficult time submitting to a boss with a certain personality, God may call us to continue working with someone who has the same personality until we master the situation in a godly way. God does not want us to be on the run; He wants us to confront our fears and frustrations in order to find peace in Him.

In 1 Kings 19, Elijah was running away when God told him to go back and finish what God had told him to do. When Jonah ran from his problems, he wound up in a whale's belly. When God delivered him from the whale, He told him to go back to Nineveh and deliver His message to the people there (see Jonah, chapters 1-3).

If we try to solve our own problems without waiting on God, we can make bigger messes. Sarah did this when she convinced her husband Abraham to have a child with her handmaid Hagar rather than waiting for the child promised them by God (see Genesis 16). Hagar eventually ran away because of the way Sarah was treating her, but the Angel of the Lord told her, "Go back to your mistress and [humbly] submit to her control" (v. 9). He promised to bless her obedience by giving her many descendants (see v. 10).

God may be telling you to go back to the place of your frustration and pain, and allow Him to walk you through that doorway and into victorious living. Do not run from His invitation to emotional healing.

Ways People Run from Their Problems

It is common for people to run from their problems, because they do not want to take responsibility for their actions. Most people look for the easy way out, instead of looking for the right choice. Some people physically run away from their problems, going from marriage to marriage, or job to job. Some people mentally run away from their problems through the abuse of drugs and alcohol. But problems do not disappear by avoiding them.

Every choice we make brings results. If we choose never to clean house, eventually everything in it will deteriorate. If we choose not to go to the grocery store, sooner or later we will not have any food to eat. The problem is that we want to make wrong choices and get right results, but that does not work. We always reap what we sow (see Galatians 6:7-8). If we choose to do what is right, we will consequently break the cycle of problems that come against us.

Some people run from problems by making excuses. When God tries to confront them with something, they make an excuse, saying, "Well, I am acting like this because I am tired." Or, "I act this way because I have been mistreated all my life." An excuse is a reason stuffed with a lie. The problem with excuses is that as long as we hold on to them, we will not see change.

Jesus told the story of a man who planned a great supper and invited many guests to come (see Luke 14:16-24), but one by one they made excuses for why they could not come. The first one said he was too busy with a piece of land that he had just bought. Another gave the excuse of buying oxen that needed to be examined, and another said he could not come because he had just got married. So the man invited all the poor, disabled, blind, and lame people in the streets and filled his house with people willing to be blessed. Those with excuses never tasted the great supper that had been prepared for them.

Another way people run from problems is by blaming others for everything that is wrong. Adam blamed Eve for eating the forbidden fruit; he even blamed God for giving him the woman, while Eve blamed the serpent for misleading her (see Genesis 3). The Israelites blamed Moses for their misery in the wilderness and begged to go back to their place of bondage in Egypt (see Exodus 14:10-12).

I remember when I tried to blame everybody else for my problems. Everything was Dave's fault, or the fault of my upbringing. I had to see that *I* was my only real problem.

Jesus said, "Why do you stare from without at the very

small particle that is in your brother's eye but do not become aware of *and* consider the beam of timber that is in your own eye?" (Matthew 7:3).

I enjoy a tremendous amount of freedom now, but it came through facing the truth about myself. God pointed out that I had a bad attitude, and my problems would not be solved until *I* changed. It hurt to change, but I had to face what God had revealed to me.

We will only get free by hearing the truth and doing what we hear God tell us to do. For example, if God tells you that you have a problem with jealousy, you will continue to miss out on blessings until you deal with it. You will have to start rejoicing when good things happen to other people. Whatever it is that holds you in bondage will have to be confronted with the truth before you can move on.

People also run from their problems by staying too busy. We can even get so busy doing church work that we do not take time to hear from God. I was in full-time ministry, helping people solve their problems, when God spoke to me and said, "Joyce you are so busy doing things *for* Me that you never spend any time *with* Me." I had to take an honest look at my time and stop doing many things that were not bearing fruit. Staying busy was helping me avoid issues I needed to deal with.

Paul prayed that we, the Church, would learn to sense what is vital:

> And this I pray: that your love may abound yet more and more *and* extend to its fullest development in knowledge and all keen insight [that your love may display itself in greater depth of acquaintance and more comprehensive discernment],
>
> So that you may surely learn to sense what is vital, *and* approve *and* prize what is excellent *and* of real value [rec-

> ognizing the highest and the best, and distinguishing the moral differences], and that you may be untainted *and* pure and unerring *and* blameless [so that with hearts sincere and certain and unsullied, you may approach] the day of Christ [not stumbling *nor* causing others to stumble]. (Philippians 1:9,10)

We need to know what to say yes to and what to turn down. I have had to learn how to say no, because I want to make every day count that I have left in this life. Many times what looks good is the enemy of the better thing that is coming.

For example, God told one woman I know that she needed to stop spending so much time helping other people instead of spending time with her own child. We need to know what God wants us to do with our time, and we learn what He wants by spending time with Him in prayer. If hearing from God is difficult for you, I encourage you to read my book titled *How to Hear from God*. In it I share many ways that God communicates with us, and how it always lines up with His Word and leads us to peace.

Procrastination is another common way to run from problems. We make excuses, blame others, and say we are too busy, and so we put off doing something God has told us to do. We think we will do it later, but later never comes. We "delay or turn a deaf ear," just as Isaiah warned in chapter 1, verse 23.

Haggai 1:2-7 shows what becomes of those who put off what God has told them to do:

> Thus says the Lord of hosts: These people say, The time is not yet come that the Lord's house should be rebuilt [although Cyrus had ordered it done eighteen years before].
>
> Then came the word of the Lord by Haggai the prophet, saying,

> Is it time for you yourselves to dwell in your paneled houses while this house [of the Lord] lies in ruins?
>
> Now therefore thus says the Lord of hosts: Consider your ways *and* set your mind on what has come to you.
>
> You have sown much, but you have reaped little; you eat, but you do not have enough; you drink, but you do not have your fill; you clothe yourselves, but no one is warm; and he who earns wages has earned them to put them in a bag with holes in it.
>
> Thus says the Lord of hosts: Consider your ways (your previous and present conduct) *and* how you have fared.

We have to motivate ourselves to do what God tells us to do, *when* He tells us to do it. Solomon wrote, "He who observes the wind [and waits for all conditions to be favorable] will not sow, and he who regards the clouds will not reap" (Ecclesiastes 11:4).

If you look at your circumstances, you will put off doing what God is telling you to do. It can even seem like the worst time to do whatever God says to do, but there is an anointing on "now," if God has told you to act.

It is not good to spend our time running from problems. We need to slow down, discern what is vital, accept responsibility for our actions, and if need be simply say, "I was wrong, and I am sorry." We must not let procrastination rob us of God's blessings.

If we want to enjoy God's best for our lives, we must stop making excuses, stop blaming others, and stop being too busy to do what God says to do. He may tell us to give, help, pray, forgive, apologize, or something else. But whatever it may be, we need to learn to be "now people" who hear God and act quickly when He speaks to us.

10

Redeemed and Made Righteous

JESUS CHRIST GAVE His life that we might have righteousness—or as I like to write it, RIGHTeousness. Righteousness is meant for all who believe "*with* personal trust *and* confident reliance on Jesus Christ (the Messiah)" (Romans 3:22).

Speaking of Jesus, Peter wrote, "He personally bore our sins in His [own] body on the tree [as on an altar and offered Himself on it], that we might die (cease to exist) to sin and live to righteousness. By His wounds you have been healed" (1 Peter 2:24).

We were created by God to feel right and good about ourselves. But the devil wants all of us to feel wrong about ourselves; he wants us to feel shame, guilt, and condemnation. Because of the presence of sin in the world, and the sin nature that came upon us through the fall of mankind, we cannot do everything right.

To resist the devil's temptation to live in constant regret instead of continual victory, we must know and understand the truth of God's Word. When we accept Jesus as our Savior, He imparts or *gives to us* the gift of righteousness, and *by faith*, we are made right with God. We are not made right with God because of our own perfection or good works; we are considered righteous because of our trust in Jesus Christ.

In 2 Corinthians 5:21 the apostle Paul tells us what God did for us: "For our sake He made Christ [virtually] to be sin Who knew no sin, so that in *and* through Him we might become [endued with, viewed as being in, and examples of] the righteousness of God [what we ought to be, approved and acceptable and in right relationship with Him, by His goodness]."

God sent Jesus to redeem us (that is, to buy us back from the devil to whom we had sold ourselves as slaves to sin), to restore us (to make us as we were supposed to be in the beginning). We were created and redeemed by God for righteousness, not shame, guilt, and condemnation.

No Condemnation in Christ

If we read and understand the Word of God, we can be set free from wrong thinking about ourselves. Paul wrote in Romans 8:1: "THEREFORE, [there is] now no condemnation (no adjudging guilty of wrong) for those who are in Christ Jesus, *who live [and] walk not after the dictates of the flesh, but after the dictates of the Spirit.*"

Of course, if we would follow the leading of the Holy Spirit, we would never do anything wrong, so guilt would have no place to take root in us. However, since we are human, none of us is incapable of making a mistake. As our Lord pointed out, "The spirit indeed is willing, but the flesh is weak" (Matthew 26:41 KJV).

We cannot perform perfectly, even though we would like to, but we can live free from guilt by walking in the Spirit. The Lord promises to lead us through life, if we listen to Him and obey Him: "Listen to *and* obey My voice, and I will be your God and you will be My people; and *walk in the whole way that I command you*, that it may be well with you" (Jeremiah 7:23, emphasis mine).

We sin when we stop doing what the Holy Spirit guides us to do. Condemnation and guilt feelings come as a result of that sin, because the devil sees an opening and immediately moves to rob us of our confidence in God's grace. If we ever hope to live without guilt, we must deal with the temptation to sin as soon as we are aware of it.

If you do give into temptation or fall into sin, instead of trying to restore yourself through good works, which is walking after the flesh (your human nature), ask God to forgive you and choose to turn back to the Spirit. You sin because you stop following the leading of the Holy Spirit. If you keep following the flesh, you will only get deeper and deeper into trouble and turmoil. Instead, turn back quickly to following the Spirit, allowing Him to lead and guide you in correcting your situation.

The Spirit always has the correct answer for every problem—and He will not condemn you when you return to Him. It is written: "For God has not appointed us to [incur His] wrath [He did not select us to condemn us], but [that we might] obtain [His] salvation through our Lord Jesus Christ (the Messiah)" (1 Thessalonians 5:9).

For example, the Spirit will lead us to repentance, which produces forgiveness from God: "If we [freely] admit that we have sinned *and* confess our sins, He is faithful and just (true to His own nature and promises) and will forgive our sins [dismiss our lawlessness] and [continuously] cleanse us from all unrighteousness [everything not in conformity to His will in purpose, thought, and action]" (1 John 1:9).

Following the flesh will lead to works that supposedly win the right to receive God's favor. But the flesh always attempts to repay for mistakes rather than simply receive God's gift of pardon and restoration.

Dealing with Guilt

The Lord once gave me a great revelation about guilt. I had felt guilty as long as I could remember. Guilt was my constant companion. We went everywhere together! This sin-consciousness began early in my childhood when I was being sexually abused. Even though my father told me that what he was doing to me was not wrong, it made me feel dirty and guilty. Of course, as I got older and became aware that it was wrong, but had no way to make it stop, the guilt continued and increased.

I learned firsthand that guilt is an unbearable burden, a heaviness that depresses the spirit. Guilt makes everything seem dark and makes us feel tired and weary. Actually it drains our energy and saps the strength we need to resist sin and Satan. So the result is that guilt and condemnation actually increase sin.

I believe that I was addicted to guilt. Before I learned about God's grace, I can never remember being guilt-free! Even if I was not doing anything particularly bad or sinful, I found something to feel wrong about.

Satan wants to press us down. He is the accuser of those who believe in Christ; he continues to bring charges against us before God (see Revelation 12:10). But David, the psalmist, wrote, "You, O Lord, are a shield for me, my glory, and the lifter of my head" (Psalm 3:3).

For example, I was shopping one day, and my ever-present companion of guilt was with me. I do not recall what I had done wrong this time; it does not even matter, it was always something. I was about to get out of my car and go into a store when the Holy Spirit said to me, "Joyce, how do you plan to get forgiveness for this sin?"

I knew the right answer. I said, "I'll accept the sacrifice Jesus made for me when He died at Calvary." We can know the right answer (have head knowledge), and still not apply it to our own situation.

Then the Holy Spirit continued: "I see, Joyce, and *when* do you plan to accept Jesus' sacrifice?"

A major revelation began to shine forth in me! At that moment I knew that I could wait two or three days until I felt guilty long enough and then accept God's forgiveness, or I could receive that pardon right then.

I always asked for forgiveness for my sins right away, but I never accepted it until I felt that I had suffered enough to pay for it. God revealed to me what I was doing, how much unnecessary pain I was causing myself. He even showed me that what I was doing was insulting to Jesus, that in essence I was saying, "Lord, the sacrifice of Your life and blood was good, but not good enough. I must add my work of feeling guilty before I can be forgiven."

That very day I began getting free from guilt and condemnation. I encourage you to do the same. Remember: Guilt does no good at all! It accomplishes nothing, except the following:

- Guilt drains your energy and can even make you physically or mentally ill.
- Guilt blocks your fellowship with God. Hebrews 4:15-16 says, "For we do not have a High Priest Who is unable to understand *and* sympathize *and* have a shared feeling with our weaknesses *and* infirmities *and* liability to the

assaults of temptation, but One Who has been tempted in every respect as we are, yet without sinning. Let us then fearlessly *and* confidently *and* boldly draw near to the throne of grace (the throne of God's unmerited favor to us sinners), that we may receive mercy [for our failures] and find grace to help in good time for every need [appropriate help and well-timed help, coming just when we need it]."

- Guilt, as a work of the flesh, demands that you try to pay for your sin.
- Guilt drains your spiritual energy. It leaves you weak and unable to resist new attacks from the enemy. Successful spiritual warfare requires wearing of the "breastplate of *right*eousness" (Ephesians 6:14 KJV, emphasis mine). Guilt causes you to sin more.
- Guilt exerts such tremendous pressure on you, suggesting that getting along with others is difficult. It is nearly impossible to live under a burden of guilt and still operate in the fruit of the Spirit (see Galatians 5:22, 23).

Surely you can see from this list that guilt is a good thing to give up. Let it go! It is from the devil and is intended to prevent you from ever enjoying your life or your relationship with the Lord.

If you have a serious problem in this area of guilt, you may need to ask someone to pray for you. If your faith is strong enough, pray for yourself. However, guilt steals faith; if you have lived for a long time buried under a load of guilt and condemnation, your faith may need to be strengthened. Get the help you need. Refuse to live any longer pressed down under a burden of guilt and condemnation.[6]

What about Shame?

Now that we have a better understanding of guilt, let's turn our attention to the subject of shame.

There is a shame that is normal and healthy. If I lose or break something that belongs to someone else, I feel ashamed of my mistake. I wish I had not been so careless or negligent. I am sorry, but I can ask for forgiveness, receive it, and then go on with my life. Healthy shame reminds us that we are human beings with weaknesses and limitations.

In Genesis 2:25 we read that Adam and Eve were naked in the Garden of Eden, and they were not ashamed. Besides the fact that they were not wearing any clothes, I believe this verse means that they were totally open and honest with each other, hiding behind no masks, playing no games. They were completely free to be themselves because they had no sense of shame. Once they had sinned, however, they went and hid themselves (see Genesis 3:6-8).

People should be able to enjoy perfect freedom with each other and with God, but very few are able to do so. Most people pretend. They produce false personalities and hide behind them. They act as if they are not hurt when they are, or they pretend that they do not need anyone when they do.

There is a poisonous shame that can drastically affect the quality of a person's life. This occurs when an individual who is being abused or mistreated in some way begins to internalize the shame he feels. He is no longer just ashamed of what is being done to him, but he becomes ashamed of himself because of what he is being subjected to.

Such an individual takes the shame into himself where it actually becomes the core of his being. Everything in his life becomes poisoned by his emotions so that he develops into a shame-based person.

At one time I was shame-based, but I did not know I was

ashamed of myself. I was seeing the results of shame in my life, but was unsuccessfully trying to deal with the fruit of it rather than the root.

The implied definition of the word translated *ashamed* in the *King James Version* of Genesis 2:25 is: to *be disappointed*, or *delayed* . . . confounded."[7]

This word *confounded* simply means to be frustrated or confused. *Webster's New World Dictionary* defines the verb *confound* as: "confuse"; "bewilder"; "damn."[8] Webster defines the verb *damn* as: "to condemn to an unhappy fate"; "doom"; "to criticize adversely"; "to cause the ruin of"; "make fail."[9]

If you will take the time to really study these definitions, you may discover that the root of your problem is shame.

Dealing with Shame

My life was filled with confusion because I was trying desperately to do right (so I could "feel right"), but no matter how hard I tried, I always failed. It seemed as if I were doomed to failure. I did not fail at everything, however. I was successful in the corporate world, and in a few other areas, but I was a failure at godly behavior. I always felt defeated because no matter what I accomplished on the outside, I still felt bad about myself on the inside.

I was ashamed of me!

I did not like who I was. I did not like my basic personality. I was continually rejecting my real self and trying to be someone or something I was not and never could be. (I will discuss this topic more fully in another chapter.)

Multiplied thousands of Christians spend their entire lives in this pitiful condition—living far, far below their rightful position as heirs of God and joint-heirs with Jesus Christ. I know, because I was one of them.

Paul wrote that the suffering we endure now will one day be worth the glory of the inheritance due to us:

> And if we are [His] children, then we are [His] heirs also: heirs of God and fellow heirs with Christ [sharing His inheritance with Him]; only we must share His suffering if we are to share His glory.
>
> [But what of that?] For I consider that the sufferings of this present time (this present life) are not worth being compared with the glory that is about to be revealed to us *and* in us *and* for us *and* conferred on us! (Romans 8:17-18)

It was a great day when the Holy Spirit led me to understand that shame was the source of many of my problems! There are promises in the Word of God that assure us that we can be delivered from a sense of shame. For example, it is written in Isaiah 61:7: "Instead of your [former] shame you shall have a twofold recompense; instead of dishonor *and* reproach [your people] shall rejoice in their portion. Therefore in their land they shall possess double [what they had forfeited]; everlasting joy shall be theirs."

Let's examine more closely this passage, which offers "a twofold recompense." A *recompense* is a reward or compensation for injury. In other words, if you trust God and do things His way, He will see to it that you are repaid for every injustice ever done to you. You will receive double what you have forfeited or lost, and everlasting joy will be yours! That is a wonderful promise, and I can vouch for the reality of it. God has done that very thing for me, and He will do it for you too.

Another promise from the Lord is found in Isaiah 54:4: "Fear not, for you shall not be ashamed; neither be confounded *and* depressed, for you shall not be put to shame. For you shall forget the shame of your youth, and you shall not [seriously] remember the reproach of your widowhood any more."

How inspiring and encouraging it is to know that you will forget the harm of your past and will never have to seriously remember those hard, hard times! This is even a promise that you can stand on if you are still being abused or mistreated.

Perhaps you feel that the Lord has told you to endure for a season some verbal or emotional abuse while He is doing a work in the person who is hurting you. How can you protect yourself from developing a shame-based nature? The prayer of the psalmist can be yours also: "O keep me, Lord, and deliver me; let me not be ashamed *or* disappointed, for my trust *and* my refuge are in You" (Psalm 25:20).

God can keep you from shame. I suggest that every time you suffer from verbal or emotional abuse, simply pray and ask God to keep you from the shame that tries to build up within you. Use this word in Psalm 25:20 as a double-edged sword against the enemy (which in this case is shame).

Following is an example of how this approach will work for your benefit. I know a pastor's wife who has no problems at all in her sexual relations with her husband, even though relatives sexually abused her for many years. On the other hand, as a result of my sexual abuse, I had many, many problems to confront and overcome in my sexual relations with my husband.

What made the difference? While questioning my friend, I discovered that throughout her childhood she had maintained a strong faith in God. The abuse began when she was about fourteen years of age. By that time she had already enjoyed many years of good Christian fellowship and an active prayer life. She prayed each time her abusers molested her, asking God to cover her so it would not affect her sexual relationship with her future husband. She knew that one day she was going to marry a pastor because the Lord had already revealed it to her. Her prayers protected her from shame and bondage in that area.

In my case, I did not know enough about God to activate my faith through prayer. Therefore I did suffer from shame—until I discovered that I was shame-based and learned about God's promise to deliver me.

You can also be delivered from shame, which is the source of many complex inner problems, such as:

- Alienation
- Compulsive behaviors (drug/alcohol/substance abuse; eating disorders; addiction to money, work, or other objects or activities; sexual perversions; excessive need to be in control; lack of self-control or self-discipline; gossiping; judgmental spirit; etc.)
- Depression
- Deep sense of inferiority ("There-is-something-wrong-with-me" thinking)
- Failure syndrome
- Isolating loneliness
- Lack of confidence
- Neurotic behavior (A neurotic person assumes too much responsibility; in times of conflict he automatically presumes that he is at fault.)
- Perfectionism
- Timidity (fear of all types)
- Inability to develop and maintain healthy relationships

Depression

What we believe in our heart about ourselves deeply influences how we act: "For as he [a person] thinks in his heart, so is he" (Proverbs 23:7, paraphrased). If we think poorly of ourselves, we will be depressed.

Extreme numbers of people suffer from this terrible condition of depression, which has many complex causes, one of which is shame. If you are prone to depression, it may be a sign of a deeper problem—a root of shame.

Those who are shame-based think and speak negatively about themselves. Such wrong thinking and speaking places a heavy weight on the spirit. This is a major problem because God created human beings for righteousness, love, and acceptance. God is always pouring forth these virtues upon His children, but many of His children do not know how to receive them.

You cannot receive love and acceptance from God if you are against yourself. If you have a problem in this area, do not just sit by and allow the devil to destroy you. Confront your spiritual enemy with spiritual action. Change your thinking and your speaking. Begin purposely to think and say only good things about yourself. Make a list of your best qualities and what the Word says about you, and confess it several times a day.

Meditate on truths from God's Word such as: "For our sake He made Christ [virtually] to be sin Who knew no sin, so that in *and* through Him we might become [endued with, viewed as being in, and examples of] the righteousness of God [what we ought to be, approved and acceptable and in right relationship with Him, by His goodness]" (2 Corinthians 5:21). Then say, "I am the righteousness of God in Christ."

Say out loud "God loves me" when you read, "For God so greatly loved *and* dearly prized the world that He [even] gave up His only begotten (unique) Son, so that whoever believes in (trusts in, clings to, relies on) Him shall not perish (come to destruction, be lost) but have eternal (everlasting) life" (John 3:16).

Read Romans 12:6-8: "Having gifts (faculties, talents, qualities) that differ according to the grace given us, let us use them: [He whose gift is] prophecy, [let him prophesy] according to the proportion of his faith; [he whose gift is] practical service, let him give himself to serving; he who teaches, to his teaching; he who exhorts (encourages), to his exhortation; he who contributes, let him do it in simplicity *and* liberality; he who gives aid *and* superintends, with zeal *and* singleness of mind; he who does acts of mercy, with genuine cheerfulness *and* joyful eagerness." Then confess, "I have gifts and abilities given to me by the Lord."

Ponder in your heart the words of the Lord when He said, "Because you are precious in My sight and honored, and because I love you, I will give men in return for you and peoples in exchange for your life" (Isaiah 43:4). Rejoice as you admit, "I am precious and valuable to God."

Search the Word of God for other positive confessions about yourself.

Another wise practice is to get a thorough medical examination to rule out the possibility of any physical condition that may be affecting your mental and emotional outlook. Unless your depression is caused by some health problem, it can usually be traced to negative thinking and speaking. Even when the depression is caused by some physical condition (hormonal or chemical imbalance, etc.), the devil will take advantage of the situation. He will offer many negative thoughts, which, if received and meditated upon, will only make the problem seem many times worse than it actually is.

I repeat: When you feel depressed, check your thinking. It is not God's will for you to be depressed. Align your thoughts with the Word of God. Isaiah 61:3 says that the Lord has given us "the garment [expressive] of praise instead of a heavy, burdened, *and* failing spirit." Nehemiah said, "The joy of the Lord is your strength *and* stronghold" (8:10). Believe what the Word says you are, and that is what you will become. Believe what the devil says you are, and you will become that. The choice is yours: "therefore choose life, that you and your descendants may live" (Deuteronomy 30:19).

11

Self-Rejection or Self-Acceptance

SHAME CAUSES SELF-REJECTION and, in some cases, self-hatred. In more extreme cases, it can develop into self-abuse, including self-mutilation. I have ministered to several people who have shown me scars on their bodies from their cutting, burning, or biting themselves, as well as bruises from their beating or hitting themselves, and bald spots from their pulling out their own hair.

Some people even starve themselves as a form of punishment. Others behave in an obnoxious manner so they will be rejected. Since they have rejected themselves, they are convinced that others will also reject them, so they manifest behavior in accordance with what they believe about themselves. The list of potential problems goes on and on, but I am sure you see the point I am making:

You cannot get beyond your own opinion of yourself–no matter how many good things God may say about you in His

Word. Regardless of all the wonderful plans God may have for your life, none of them will come to pass without your cooperation.

You need to believe what God says.

Accept God's Opinion of You

If you are seeking recovery from abuse, you must not allow other people's opinions of you, as evidenced by the way you have been mistreated in the past, to determine your worth. Remember, people who feel worthless always try to find something wrong with you so they can feel a little better about themselves. Keep in mind that this is their problem, not yours.

In John 3:18, the Lord Jesus states that no one who believes in Him will *ever* be rejected by Him or His heavenly Father. If God accepts you because of your faith in His Son Jesus Christ, then you can stop rejecting yourself and let your healing process continue.

It may be that you are not totally rejecting yourself, but only parts of yourself that are displeasing to you. In my own case, I rejected my personality. I did not understand that I had a divine calling on my life to full-time ministry and that God designed my basic temperament for what He had for me to do.

My personality was flawed, of course, due to the years of abuse I had suffered, and was in need of Holy Spirit adjustment, but it was still the basic personality that God had chosen for me. However, because I did not understand that fact, I thought I had to become totally different. I was constantly trying to be someone else, which was not God's will for me—nor is it His will that you become someone else.

Remember: God will help you be all *you* can be—all you were originally designed to be. But He will never permit you to be successful at becoming someone else.

The Spirit-Controlled Temperament

Perhaps you have observed another person—a friend or a spiritual leader—and said, "He is the way people *ought* to be" or "She is liked and accepted by *everyone*." You may have even tried to be like that individual without consciously planning to do so.

Of course, other people can be good examples to us, but even if we pattern ourselves after their good qualities, it must still be our own personal "flavor" of those good traits that characterizes us.

I have a bold, straightforward, decisive, take-charge personality. God instilled that type of nature in me to help me fulfill His call upon my life. However, for many, many years I struggled and lived in frustration because I kept trying to be more timid, mild, gentle, quiet, and sweet. I tried desperately not to be so assertive and aggressive.

The truth is that I vainly tried to model myself after my pastor's wife, my husband, and various friends whom I respected and admired. My efforts only resulted in increased frustration, which made me even more difficult to get along with. I needed to learn to quit trying to be like others and simply become "the best *me I* could be." Yes, I did need change. I did need more of the fruit of the Spirit—especially kindness, gentleness, and meekness—because I was too hard, harsh, and abrasive. But once I learned to accept my basic, God-given temperament, then I was able to let the Holy Spirit begin to change me into what He wanted me to be.

Once we quit striving to be like others, then the Spirit is able to use our strengths and to control our weaknesses. Then we begin to develop a "Spirit-controlled temperament." This temperament is explained in Galatians 5:22-25:

> But the fruit of the [Holy] Spirit [the work which His presence within accomplishes] is love, joy (gladness), peace, patience (an even temper, forbearance), kindness, goodness (benevolence), faithfulness,
>
> Gentleness (meekness, humility), self-control (self-restraint, continence). Against such things there is no law [that can bring a charge].
>
> And those who belong to Christ Jesus (the Messiah) have crucified the flesh (the godless human nature) with its passions and appetites *and* desires.
>
> If we live by the [Holy] Spirit, let us also walk by the Spirit. [If by the Holy Spirit we have our life in God, let us go forward walking in line, our conduct controlled by the Spirit.]

Many years have passed since I finally learned that I had to accept and love myself, not hate and reject myself. I have since discovered the secret to developing the Spirit-controlled temperament. The key is spending quality personal time with the Lord and receiving help from Him on a regular basis.

Strengthened in the Inner Man

I still have weaknesses in my natural man; however, as long as I abide in the Lord, seeking Him first, He continually imparts to me the power I need to manifest my strengths and not my weaknesses.

The apostle Paul prayed that the believers would be strengthened "in the inner man," that the Holy Spirit would indwell their innermost being and personality:

> May He grant you out of the rich treasury of His glory to be strengthened *and* reinforced with mighty power in the inner

man by the [Holy] Spirit [Himself indwelling your innermost being and personality].

May Christ through your faith [actually] dwell (settle down, abide, make His permanent home) in your hearts! May you be rooted deep in love *and* founded securely on love,

That you may have the power *and* be strong to apprehend *and* grasp with all the saints [God's devoted people, the experience of that love] what is the breadth and length and height and depth [of it];

[That you may really come] to know [practically, through experience for yourselves] the love of Christ, which far surpasses mere knowledge [without experience]; that you may be filled [through all your being] unto all the fullness of God [may have the richest measure of the divine Presence, and become a body wholly filled and flooded with God Himself]! (Ephesians 3:16-19)

This is our great need, to be strengthened in our "inner man" by the presence of God Himself. God told Paul, "My grace (My favor and loving-kindness and mercy) is enough for you [sufficient against any danger and enables you to bear the trouble manfully]; for My strength *and* power are made perfect (fulfilled and completed) *and show themselves most effective* in [your] weakness" (2 Corinthians 12:9).

God's strength is made perfect in our weakness. This means that when we are weak in a certain area, we do not have to hate or reject ourselves because of it. Like Paul, we have the great privilege of admitting our weaknesses and asking the Holy Spirit to control them.

In my flesh, I still have a tendency to be sharp, rude, and blunt. By the grace, strength, and power of the Lord, however, I am able to manifest "the fruit of the Spirit" and to be kind, pleasant, understanding, and longsuffering.

That does not mean that I never fail. Like everyone else, I slip and make mistakes. But I have come to understand that I do not have to be perfect in order to receive acceptance, love, and help from the Lord. Neither do you.

God is *for* you! He wants *you* to be for *you*. The devil is *against* you, and he wants *you* to be against *you*.

Are you for yourself or against yourself? Are you cooperating with God's plan for your life, or with the devil's plan for you? Are you in agreement with God or with the enemy?

Accepted in the Beloved

God chose us as His beloved, adopted children, setting us apart as His own:

> Even as [in His love] He chose us [actually picked us out for Himself as His own] in Christ before the foundation of the world, that we should be holy (consecrated and set apart for Him) and blameless in His sight, *even* above reproach, before Him in love.
>
> For He foreordained us (destined us, planned in love for us) to be adopted (revealed) as His own children through Jesus Christ, in accordance with the purpose of His will [because it pleased Him and was His kind intent]—
>
> [So that we might be] to the praise *and* the commendation of His glorious grace (favor and mercy), which He so freely bestowed on us in the Beloved. (Ephesians 1:4-6)

In Exodus 19:5, the Lord tells His people that they are His own "peculiar possession and treasure." That word applies to us today as much as it did to the children of Israel. In John 3:18, Jesus told Nicodemus that no one who believes in Him will ever be condemned (rejected). You may not feel treasured, or even acceptable, but you are. In Ephesians 1:6 KJV, Paul says that all of us who believe in Christ have been "accepted in the beloved." That should give us a sense of personal value and worth.

I remember standing in a prayer line where I overheard a woman next to me telling the pastor who was ministering to her how much she hated and despised herself. The pastor became very firm with her and in a strong manner rebuked her, saying, "Who do you think you are? You have no right to hate yourself. God paid a high price for you and your freedom. He loved you so much that He sent His only Son to die for you . . . to suffer in your place. You have no right to hate or reject yourself. Your part is to receive what Jesus died to give you!"

The woman was shocked. I was shocked too, just listening. Yet sometimes it takes a strong word to get us to realize the trap that Satan has set for us.

Self-rejection and self-hatred can almost seem pious in a sense. They can become a way of punishing ourselves for our mistakes, failures, and inabilities. We cannot be perfect, so we reject and despise ourselves.

I ask you to think of these prophetic words in Isaiah 53:3, which describe our Lord Jesus Christ: "He was despised and rejected *and* forsaken by men, a Man of sorrows *and* pains, and acquainted with grief *and* sickness; and like One from Whom men hide their faces He was despised, and we did not appreciate His worth *or* have any esteem for Him."

Do you lack appreciation for your own value and worth? Surely, you are valuable; otherwise your heavenly Father would not have paid such a heavy price for your redemption.

Isaiah 53:4-5 goes on to say that Christ "has borne our griefs (sicknesses, weaknesses, and distresses) and carried our sorrows *and* pains [of punishment], yet we [ignorantly] considered Him stricken, smitten, and afflicted by God [as if with leprosy]. But He was wounded for our transgressions, He was bruised for our guilt *and* iniquities; the chastisement [needful to obtain] peace *and* well-being for us was upon Him, and with the stripes [that wounded] Him we are healed *and* made whole."

The "healing package" purchased by Jesus with His blood is available to all who will believe and receive. That package includes the healing of the emotions as well as the body. If a person has done wrong, justice demands rejection, despising, and condemnation. However, Jesus bore all that for us, just as He bore our sins. What a glorious truth!

Since Jesus bore your sins on the cross, along with the hatred, rejection, and condemnation they deserved, you do not have to reject or hate yourself anymore.

The day I started our ministry, I asked God, "What do You want me to teach at the first meeting?"

He said, "I want you to tell My people that I love them."

I argued, "Oh, I want a message of power." That's what I said! I wanted to be God's woman of power for the hour. I wanted something that would just stun people with great revelation. I said, "Everybody knows You love them. I can't go preach John 3:16."

He said, "No, very few of My people know that I love them. If they did, they would act a whole lot different than what they do."

The Bible says, "There is no fear in love [dread does not exist], but full-grown (complete, perfect) love turns fear out of doors *and* expels every trace of terror! For fear brings with it the thought of punishment, and [so] he who is afraid has not reached the full maturity of love [is not yet grown into love's complete perfection]. We love *Him*, because He first loved us" (1 John 4:18-19). I understood that if God's people knew how much He loved them, they would not be fearful. If they knew the love of God, they would not run from Him, they would run *to* Him.

So for a year after that first teaching, I meditated on the love of God. I would drive in my car saying, "God *loves* me. God loves *me*. He loves me, *me*. The Creator of the universe loves *me*." The first book that I wrote was a result of spending this year of focus on God's love. It is called *Tell Them I Love Them*.

Once you understand that God loves you, you can love yourself in a balanced way. Look at yourself in the mirror and say to yourself, "God loves you." Receive and accept yourself; tell yourself frequently, "I accept you."

After saying, "You shall love the Lord your God," Jesus added, "You shall love your neighbor as yourself. There is no other commandment greater than these" (Mark 12:30-31). If you cannot get along with or love yourself, you will find it too difficult to get along with or love anyone else. Let the healing love of God do a work in your life.

Give yourself a hug sometimes, simply as a reminder that God loves you, and therefore you are lovable. Wrap your arms around yourself and say: "I no longer reject myself! Instead, I accept myself in Christ. I love myself, not selfishly but in a balanced way. I am not perfect, but with the help of the Lord I am improving day by day."

What about Rejection from Others?

Most likely, sooner or later, you will experience some form of rejection. Not everybody will like you. Some people may even aggressively dislike you. It is extremely helpful that you develop a mature attitude in this area.

We know that Jesus increased in wisdom and stature, and in favor with God and man (see Luke 2:52). In my own case, I ask God for favor with Him and with people, and I believe that He provides it. I suggest that you do the same. Here is a prayer to help you achieve an acceptable attitude:

Today, Lord, I am going to do my best, with Your help, and for Your glory. I realize that there are many different people in the world with a variety of opinions and expectations. I probably will not please all of them all of the time. I will concentrate on being a God-pleaser and not a self-pleaser or a man-pleaser. The rest I leave in Your hands, Lord. Grant me favor with You and with men, and continue transforming me into the image of Your dear Son. Thank You, Lord.

No one enjoys being rejected, but all of us can learn to handle rejection and get on with our lives, if we remember that Jesus was also rejected and despised. He gained the victory over rejection by being faithful to God's plan for His life.

Rejection from other people wounds our emotions. It certainly hurts, and yet, for our own sake, we must remember that, if we are born again, the Helper (the Holy Spirit) lives in us to strengthen, undergird, and comfort us.

I think we spend valuable time and energy trying to avoid being rejected. We become "pleasers of men" (see Ephesians 6:6; Colossians 3:22). After all, we reason, if we can keep everyone else happy, they will not reject us.

To avoid pain, some of us build walls around ourselves so we will not get hurt, but that is pointless. God has shown me that it is impossible to live in this world if we are not willing to get hurt. People are not perfect; therefore they hurt and disappoint us, just as we hurt and disappoint others.

I have a wonderful husband, but occasionally he has hurt me. Because I came from such a painful background, the moment that kind of thing happened, I used to put up walls to protect myself. *After all*, I reasoned, *no one can hurt me if I don't let anyone get close to me*. However, I learned that if I wall others out, I also wall myself in.

The Lord has shown me that He wants to be my Protector, but He cannot do that if I am busy trying to protect myself. He has not promised that I will *never* get hurt, but He has promised to heal me if I come to Him rather than try to take care of everything myself.

If you build walls around yourself out of fear, then you must tear them down out of faith. Go to Jesus with each old wound and receive His healing grace. When someone hurts you, take that new wound to Jesus. Do not let it fester. Take it to the Lord and be willing to handle it His way and not your own.

Receive this scripture as a personal promise from the Lord to you: "For I will restore health to you, and I will heal your wounds, says the Lord, because they have called you an outcast, saying, This is Zion, whom no one seeks after *and* for whom no one cares!" (Jeremiah 30:17).

Confess with the psalmist: "Although my father and my mother have forsaken me, yet the Lord will take me up [adopt me as His child]" (Psalm 27:10).

With the help of the Lord, you can survive rejection and find your completion "in Him."

12

Rejection's Effect on Relationships

A PERSON WHO has a root of rejection in his life is usually handicapped in relationships. In order to sustain healthy, loving, lasting relationships, a person must not fear rejection. When this fear becomes the motivating factor in the life of an individual, he will spend his time trying to avoid rejection rather than building healthy relationships.

Nobody goes through life totally escaping moments of feeling rejected. Everyone experiences some rejection. However, if there has been enough of it to leave scars, it may cause the individual not only to function abnormally in his relationship with others, but also in his relationship with God.

He may come to believe that he is loved *conditionally*. Feeling that he must earn the love of others, he may devote his life to trying to please them. He may fear that if he does not please them, they will withdraw their love from him, reject him, or even abandon him.

Memory of the pain of such experiences often prevents personal liberty in relationships. People who have a fear of rejection, and the resulting loneliness and abandonment, usually end up allowing themselves to be controlled and manipulated by others. Since they believe that acceptance is based on performance, they are consumed with *doing* rather than *being*. Because they are afraid of simply being themselves, they spend their lives pretending—pretending to like people they detest, pretending they enjoy going places and doing things they hate, pretending that everything is fine when it is not. Such people live in continual misery because they are afraid to be honest enough to confront the real issues of life.

PRETENDING! PRETENDING! PRETENDING!

Since people who fear rejection do not believe that they are lovable in themselves, often they will use the world's standards (money, status, clothes, natural talents, etc.) to prove to themselves and others that they are valuable. They live a life of misery, always trying to prove that they have worth and value.

No matter how much outward success a person may enjoy, he is not truly successful unless he knows who he is in Christ. Philippians 3:3 exhorts us to "exult *and* glory *and* pride ourselves in Jesus Christ, and put no confidence *or* dependence [on what we are] in the flesh *and* on outward privileges *and* physical advantages *and* external appearances." It is important to remember that appearance is only the way we look, not the way we really are.

A person who is rejection-based is unable to receive love even when it is being freely offered to him. If he is able to accept love at all, it is only when he believes that he has earned it by behaving perfectly.

I remember a woman who once worked for my husband and me. She had grown up in an atmosphere of performance-based acceptance. When she did well in school, her father showed her love; when she did not do as well as he expected, he withheld his love from her. He behaved this way not only with his daughter but with other family members as well; therefore she learned that love was given as a reward for perfect performance and withheld as punishment for mistakes.

Like most people, she grew up not even realizing that her feelings and belief systems were in error. She assumed that all relationships were handled in this same way. Since she was an employee of our ministry, there were occasions when I would ask her how her work was progressing, if she had everything caught up, or if there was any job that she had been given that she was unable to get finished.

I began to notice that whenever I inquired about anything that this woman had not yet completed, she would begin to act very strangely. She would withdraw from me, avoid talking with me, and appear to work at a frenzied pace—all of which made me feel uncomfortable. Actually, I felt *rejected.*

I knew that as her employer I was entitled to the privilege of asking about her workload without having to go through a traumatic ordeal each time. So I finally confronted her about the situation, which only caused our relationship to become more strained and confused. It was obvious that neither of us really understood the root of the problem.

This was a woman who truly loved the Lord. She was intensely serious about her relationship with Him, so the situation provoked her to pray and ask God for some answers about her behavior. Too often we blame our bad behavior on someone else instead of seeking the Lord to get to the root of the problem so we can be set free.

The woman received a revelation from God that changed her entire life. The Lord showed her that because her father had rejected her when she did not perform perfectly, she mistakenly believed that everyone else was the same way. If any of her work was not fully completed by the time I inquired about it, she was convinced that I was rejecting her because I no longer loved her; therefore she withdrew from me. *I had not stopped loving her, but she had stopped receiving my love*, and so I too ended up feeling rejected.

We often do this same thing with the Lord. His love for us is not based on anything we do or do not do. In Romans 5:8, Paul tells us that God loved us when we were still in sin; that is, when we did not know Him at all—or even care.

God's love is *always* flowing to all those who will receive it. But like this employee who could not receive my love, often we reject God's love when we feel that we do not deserve it because our performance is less than perfect.

Fear of Being Rejected Causes Rejection of Others

If you cannot believe that you are basically a lovable, valuable person, you will be unable to trust others who claim they love you. If you believe that you must be perfect to be worthy of love and acceptance, then you are a candidate for a miserable life, because you will never be perfect as long as you are in an earthly body.

You may have a perfect heart, in that your desire is to please God in all things, but your performance will not match your heart's desire until you get to heaven. You can improve all the time and keep pressing toward the mark of perfection, but *you will always need Jesus as long as you are here on this earth.* There will never come a time when you will not need His forgiveness and His cleansing blood.

Unless you accept your value and worth by faith through

Christ, you will always be insecure and unable to trust those who want to love you. People who have no capacity to trust suspect the motives of others. I know this is true because I had a real problem in this area. Even when other people told me they loved me, I was always waiting for them to hurt me, disappoint me, fail me, or abuse me. I figured that they must be after something; otherwise, they would not be nice to me. I just could not believe that anyone would want me just for myself. There had to be some other reason!

I felt so bad about myself, was so full of shame, condemnation, self-hatred, and self-rejection, that whenever anyone tried to show me love and acceptance, I thought to myself, *Well, if this person likes me now, he won't when he gets to know the real me*. Therefore I would not *receive* love from other people, or from God. I deflected it by my behavior, which became more and more obnoxious as I set out to prove to everyone that I was as unlovable as I believed myself to be.

Whatever you believe about yourself on the inside is what you will manifest on the outside. If you feel unlovely and unlovable, that is how you will behave. In my case, I believed that I was not lovable, so that is how I acted. I was very difficult to get along with. I believed that other people would eventually reject me, and so they usually did. Because my attitude was manifested in my actions, I could not sustain healthy, loving, lasting relationships.

The "Prove-You-Love-Me" Syndrome

Whenever anyone did try to love me, I heaped great pressure on that person to prove it to me—continually! I needed a fresh fix of positive "strokes" every day just to maintain a good feeling about myself. I had to constantly be complimented about everything I did; otherwise, I felt rejected. If I did not receive the reinforcement I craved, then I felt unloved.

I also had to have my way about everything. As long as other people agreed with me and gave in to my desires, I felt good about myself. However, if anyone disagreed with me or denied my requests, even to the slightest degree, it prompted an emotional reaction causing me to feel rejected and unloved.

I placed impossible demands on those who did love me. I frustrated them. I was never satisfied with what they were giving me. I could not allow them to be honest with me or to confront me. My entire focus was on me, and I expected everyone else's focus to be on me also. I was actually looking to people for my sense of self-worth, which is something that only God can give.

I have since learned that my sense of worth and value are in Christ, and not in things or other people. Until I learned that truth, however, I was very unhappy and totally incapable of maintaining healthy relationships.

Receiving the love of God is a key factor in emotional healing, as I mentioned in an earlier chapter. Once a person genuinely comes to believe that God, Who is perfect, loves him in his imperfection, then he can begin to believe that other people might love him also. Trust begins to develop, and he is able to accept the love that is being offered to him.

Since I have believed and received God's love for me, my most basic needs for love and a sense of self-worth have been met. I no longer require other people to keep me "fixed" all the time, that is, feeling secure about myself. Like everyone else, I do have needs that I want people to meet; we all need encouragement, exhortation, and edification. But now there is no need to look to other people for affirmation of my value.

Now if my husband fails to compliment me on something I have done, I may be disappointed—but not devastated—because I know that I have value apart from what I do. Everyone likes to be recognized and complimented on what he does, but it is wonderful to be able to keep from falling apart if I do not receive that recognition and those compliments!

Once I learned that my value and worth are not in what I do, but in who I am in Christ, I no longer feel that I have to perform for people. I have decided that either they will or will not love me for who I am. Either way, I am secure knowing that God still loves me.

It is important to be loved for who we are and not for what we do. When we know that we have value in our identity rather than in our performance or behavior, we are able to get our minds off what others are thinking about us all the time. We can focus on them and their needs, instead of expecting their focus to be continually on us and our needs. This is the basis of healthy, loving, and lasting relationships.

13

The Confidence to Be Yourself

CONFIDENCE HAS BEEN defined as the quality of assurance that leads one to undertake something; the belief that one is able and acceptable; the certainty that causes one to be bold, open, and plain. If you think about this threefold definition, you will see why the devil attacks anyone who shows any degree of confidence.

People who have been abused, rejected, or abandoned usually lack confidence. As we have already mentioned in previous chapters, such individuals are shame-based and guilt-ridden and have a poor self-image.

The devil begins his assault on personal confidence whenever and wherever he can find an opening, especially during the vulnerable years of childhood. Even while a child is still in the womb, the devil initiates his ultimate goal of total destruction of that person. The reason is simple: An individual without confidence will never step out to do anything edifying to the kingdom of God or anything detrimental to Satan's kingdom, and therefore will never fulfill the plan of God for his life.

EXPECTED FAILURE + FEAR OF FAILURE = FAILURE

Satan does not want you to fulfill God's plan for your life because he knows that you are part of his ultimate defeat. If he can make you think and believe that you are incapable, then you will not even try to accomplish anything worthwhile. Even if you do make an effort, your fear of failure will seal your defeat, which, because of your lack of confidence, you probably expected from the beginning. This is what is often referred to as the "Failure Syndrome."

No matter how many wonderful plans God has in mind for you, there is one thing you must know: *God's ability to bring His will to pass in your life is determined by your faith in Him and in His Word.* If you truly want to be happy and successful, then you must begin to believe that God has a plan for your life and that He will cause good things to happen to you as you put your trust in Him.

The devil wants you and me to feel so bad about ourselves that we have no confidence in ourselves. But here is the good news: *We do not need confidence in ourselves—we need confidence in Jesus!*

I have confidence in myself only because I know that Christ is in me, ever present and ready to help me with everything that I attempt to do for Him. A believer without confidence is like a jumbo jet parked on the runway with no fuel; it looks good on the outside, but has no power on the inside. With Jesus inside us, we have the power to do what we could never do on our own.

Jesus died for our weaknesses and inabilities, and He is

willing to impart to us His strength and ability as we place our confidence (our faith) in Him. In John 15:5, He teaches us this important principle: "Apart from Me [cut off from vital union with Me] you can do nothing."

Once you learn this truth, when the devil lies and says, "You can't do anything right," your response to him can be, "Perhaps not, but Jesus in me can; and He will, because I am relying on Him, and not on myself. He will cause me to succeed in everything that I put my hand to" (see Joshua 1:7).

Or should the enemy say to you, "You're not able to do this, so don't even try, because you will only fail again, just as you have in the past," your response can be, "It is true that without Jesus, I am not able to do one single thing; but with Him and in Him I can do all that I need to do" (see Philippians 4:13).

Whenever the devil reminds you of your past, remind him of his future. If you read the Bible all the way through to the end, you will see that the devil's future is very bleak. Actually, he is already a defeated foe. It is written in Colossians 2:15, "[God] disarmed the principalities and powers that were ranged against us and made a bold display *and* public example of them, in triumphing over them in Him [Christ] *and* in it [the cross]" (emphasis mine).

You can resist the devil's temptation to live in fear and regret, because Jesus triumphed over his plans, and made a public display of his disgrace in the spirit realm. Satan is operating on borrowed time, and he knows it better than anybody (see Revelation 12:12). The only power he has to use against us is what we give him by believing his lies.

Always remember: *The devil* is *a liar!*

Speaking of Satan, Jesus said, "He was a murderer from the beginning and does not stand in the truth, because there is no truth in him. When he speaks a falsehood, he speaks what is natural to him, for he is a liar [himself] and the father of lies *and* of all that is false" (John 8:44).

THE LIE ABOUT SELF-CONFIDENCE

Everyone talks about self-confidence. All kinds of seminars are available on confidence, both in the secular world and the church world. Confidence is generally referred to as "self-confidence" because we all know that we need to feel good about ourselves if we are ever to accomplish anything in life. We have been taught that all people have a basic need to believe in themselves. However, that is a misconception.

Actually, we do not need to believe in ourselves—we need to believe in Jesus in us. We do not dare feel good about ourselves apart from Him. When the apostle Paul instructs us to "put no confidence in the flesh" (see Philippians 3:3), he means just what he says—do not put confidence in yourself, or in anything you can do apart from Jesus.

We do not need self-confidence; we need God-confidence!

Many people spend their whole lives climbing the ladder of success only to find that when they get to the top, their ladder was leaning against the wrong building. Others struggle, trying to behave well enough to develop a measure of confidence in themselves, only to endure repeated failures. Both of these activities produce the same results: emptiness and misery.

I have found that most people fall into one of two categories: (1) They never accomplish anything, no matter how hard they try, and end up hating themselves because of their lack of achievement, or (2) they have enough natural talent to accomplish great things, but take all the credit for their achievements, which fills them with pride. Either way, they are a failure—in the eyes of God.

The only truly successful person in God's eyes is the individual who knows he is nothing in himself, but everything in Christ. Our pride and boasting are to be in Jesus alone, and He is to have all the glory (credit due) for whatever accomplishments we may achieve.

In actuality, every person does have confidence (faith). The Bible confirms this fact in Romans 12:3. We are all born with a certain amount of faith; the important thing is where we put it. Some put their faith in themselves, some in other people, some in things—and then there are those who actually put their faith in God.

Do not be concerned about yourself, your weaknesses, or your strengths. Get your eyes off of yourself and onto the Lord. If you are weak, He can strengthen you. If you have any strength, it is because He gave it to you. So either way, your eyes should be on Him and not on yourself.

Without true confidence (in Jesus), you will create many complicated problems for yourself. Here is a partial list:

- You will never reach your full potential in Christ (as we have discussed in detail).
- Your life will be ruled by fear and filled with torment.
- You will never know true joy, fulfillment, or satisfaction.
- You will grieve the Holy Spirit Who is sent to bring God's plan to pass in your life but Who is never able to do so without your cooperation.
- You will open for yourself many doors of endless torment: self-hatred, condemnation, fear of rejection, fear of failure, fear of man, perfectionism, people-pleasing (which eliminates the possibility of being a God-pleaser), control and manipulation by others, etc.
- You will lose sight of your right to be an individual—the right to be yourself.

This last danger is the one I would like to examine now. We have looked at the others to some degree in the first part of the book, but this last one is of major importance and deserves more consideration.

Confidence to Be an Individual

In 1 Corinthians 3:16-17 and Romans 12:4-6, Paul teaches us that all of us make up one body, yet each of us is an individual member of that body. This is a truth that is very important for us to grasp because we make ourselves miserable and stifle the power of God in us when we try to be something or someone we were not designed to be.

We have often heard it said that we all came out of different molds, meaning that no two of us are exactly alike. There is nothing wrong with being different from each other! God had a purpose in creating each of us differently. If He had wanted us to be alike, He could easily have made us that way. Instead, our uniqueness was so important to Him that He even went to the extreme of giving each of us a different set of fingerprints!

Being different is not bad; it is God's plan!

We are all part of one plan, God's plan. Yet each of us has a different function, because each of us is an individual.

I define *individual* as separate, distinguished by specific attributes or identifying traits, distinct or unique.

For years I thought I was *weird*—now I know that I am *unique!* There is a big difference. If I were weird, it would indicate that something about me got messed up and did not turn out the way it should have; while my being unique indicates that there are no others like me, and therefore I have special value. You should believe that you are unique, special, and valuable.

Don't Try to Be Someone Else

One of my unique identifying traits is my voice. Most women have soft, sweet voices, but mine is deep and firm. Quite often when someone who does not know me calls our home, he will think the man of the house has answered the phone. I was not always comfortable with this very unique trait; in fact, I was insecure about it. I thought my voice was just plain weird!

When God called me to teach His Word, and I began to realize that I would one day be speaking over public address systems (loud speakers) and even have a radio and television ministry, I was terrified! I thought that surely I would be rejected because I sounded so different from the way I *thought* a woman should sound. I was comparing myself with what I perceived as normal.

Have you ever compared yourself with someone else? How did it make you feel?

We are not to compare ourselves with others, but let Jesus be our example and learn to reflect the presence and personality of the God Who indwells us.

Diamonds have many facets. God is like a flawless diamond, and each of us represents a different facet of Him. He has placed an expression of Himself in each of us, and we corporately make up His Body. What if our bodies were totally made up of mouths or ears, arms or legs? We would have no trouble speaking or hearing, carrying, or walking, but what about the other functions? What a mess we would be if it had been God's intention to make us all exactly alike.

Why is it that we struggle so much trying to be like someone else, instead of simply enjoying who we are? Because we believe the lies of the devil. We believe him, that is, until we hear the truth of God's Word, and the truth that we believe sets us free.

God's grace will never be available to you to become another person. He created you to be you—the best "*you*" you can be! Forget about trying to be someone else. That is always a mistake, because usually the person you choose to be like, the person who "has it all together," is not the way you think. Let me give you some examples:

Example One

At one point in my life I decided that my pastor's wife was the "ideal woman." She was (and still is) a sweet lady: petite, cute, blonde, soft-spoken, gentle, mild, and endowed with the gift of mercy. I, on the other hand, with my deep voice and straightforward, blunt personality, did not seem very sweet, gentle, mild, or merciful. I tried to be that way, without much success. I actually attempted to lower the volume level of my voice and change the sound of it to seem more "feminine," but I only ended up sounding phony.

This lady and I could not seem to get along. Though we wanted and tried to be friends, it just did not seem to work out. Finally, a confrontation between us revealed that I was not really enjoying her because her presence put me under pressure to be like her. The really interesting thing that we both discovered was that Satan had sold her the same pack of lies I had bought; she was struggling to be more like me! She was trying to be less fragile and more forceful, to deal with people and things more directly and with greater boldness. It is no wonder that we could not have a successful relationship—we were each being pressured by the other!

Remember this: *God said that we "shall not covet"* (Exodus 20:17)— *and that includes someone else's personality.*

Example Two

My next-door neighbor was a sweet girl who was gifted in many different ways. She sewed, had a garden and canned vegetables, played guitar and sang, did various kinds of arts and crafts, wallpapered, painted, wrote songs—in short, all the things I could not do. Since I thought I was "weird" anyway, I did not appreciate the talents I did have. I only thought about what abilities I lacked and all the things I could not do.

Since I was called by God to teach and preach His Word, my desires were different from those of many of the women I knew. While they were attending interior decorating parties, I was home praying. I was very serious about everything. It seemed to me that there was something very heavy going on inside me. While other women were relaxing and having a good time, I was constantly comparing myself to them, always feeling that something had to be wrong with me. This kind of feeling occurs when people are shame-based and insecure about who they are in Christ.

I did need to learn to "lighten up" a bit and have some fun, but God was doing something in me that needed to be done. He was causing me to see the mess that some people's lives were in, and calling me to help them out of that mess through His Word. I needed to be affected by the weight and seriousness of other people's problems.

I was in a waiting period during which God was not using me; it was a time of preparation, stretching, and growing which lasted about one full year. During that year I decided it was time for me to become what I called a "regular woman." I bought a sewing machine and took some sewing lessons. I hated it, but forced myself to continue. Sewing was not something at which I excelled either. When a person has not been gifted in an area, he is just plain no good at it.

Sewing was such a struggle for me! I kept making mistakes that caused me to feel even worse about myself. I finally managed to get through enough sewing lessons to make a few garments for my family, which they dutifully wore.

I also decided that I should grow and can tomatoes. They were just beginning to look good, almost ready to be harvested, when a swarm of bugs attacked them overnight and left huge black holes in all of them! But I was determined to can tomatoes because I had already purchased all the canning equipment. So I went to the farmers' market and bought a bushel of tomatoes! I worked and sweated, sweated and worked, until I finally got those tomatoes canned! Once again, I hated and despised every second of it, but thought I was proving that I was "regular."

Through these very painful experiences, I learned that I was miserable because God would not help me be something that He had not created me to be. I am not to be someone else—I am to be me, just as you are to be you.

Be Yourself!

You have a right to be yourself! Do not let the devil steal that right from you!

If someone you know is a good Christian example in manifesting the character of the Lord or the fruits of the Holy Spirit, you may want to follow his example. The apostle Paul said, "PATTERN YOURSELVES after me [follow my example], as I imitate *and* follow Christ (the Messiah)" (1 Corinthians 11:1). Following a person's example is entirely different from trying to be like that individual in personality or gifts.

I strongly encourage you to think this over: Are you accepting the fact that you were not created like everyone else, that you are a unique individual? Are you enjoying your uniqueness, or are you at war with yourself as I was?

So many people are waging a private war inside themselves, comparing themselves to almost everyone they come near, which causes them to judge themselves or the other person. They conclude either that they should be like other people, or that others should be like them.

Lies!

None of us should be like anyone else. Each of us should be the facet of the Lord that He intends for us to be—uniquely individual—so that corporately we may accomplish God's plan and bring glory to Him.

14

Forgiveness Frees You to Live Again

RECEIVING FORGIVENESS FOR past mistakes and sins, and forgiving others for their mistakes and sins, are two of the most important factors in emotional healing.

Forgiveness is a gift given to those who do not deserve it.

God wants to begin our process of forgiving those who have hurt us by giving us the gift of forgiveness first. When we confess our sins to Him, He forgives us of our sins, puts them away from Him as far as the East is from the West, and remembers them no more.

When you are tempted to look back, remember the promises of these scriptures:

> If we [freely] admit that we have sinned *and* confess our sins, He is faithful and just (true to His own nature and promises) and will forgive our sins [dismiss our lawlessness] and [continuously] cleanse us from all unrighteous-

ness [everything not in conformity to His will in purpose, thought, and action]. (1 John 1:9)

As far as the east is from the west, so far has He removed our transgressions from us.

As a father loves *and* pities his children, so the Lord loves *and* pities those who fear Him [with reverence, worship, and awe].

For He knows our frame, He [earnestly] remembers *and* imprints [on His heart] that we are dust. (Psalm 103:12-14)

Whereas this One [Christ], after He had offered a single sacrifice for our sins [that shall avail] for all time, sat down at the right hand of God, then to wait until His enemies should be made a stool beneath His feet.

For by a single offering He has forever completely cleansed *and* perfected those who are consecrated *and* made holy.

And also the Holy Spirit adds His testimony to us [in confirmation of this]. For having said, this is the agreement (testament, covenant) that I will set up *and* conclude with them after those days, says the Lord: I will imprint My laws upon their hearts, and I will inscribe them on their minds (on their inmost thoughts and understanding),

He then goes on to say, *And their sins and their lawbreaking I will remember no more.* (Hebrews 10:12-17, emphasis mine)

But for us to benefit from God's promised forgiveness, we must receive it by faith.

Many years ago when I was first developing my relationship with the Lord, each night I would beg His forgiveness for my past sins. One evening as I knelt beside my bed, I heard the Lord say to me, "Joyce, I forgave you the first time you asked, but you have not *received* My gift of forgiveness because you have not forgiven yourself."

Have you received God's gift of forgiveness? If you have not, and you are ready to do so, ask the Lord to forgive you for all your sins right now. Then pray this aloud:

> *I receive Your forgiveness, Lord, for the sin of*
> ______________________ *(name the sin).*

It may be difficult to verbalize some of your mistakes and sins from the past, but speaking them forth helps bring the release you need.

One time as I was praying, I asked God to forgive me because (as I put it), "I missed it."

"Missed what?" He asked.

"Well, You know, Lord," I answered, "You know what I did."

He did, indeed, know. But for my sake it was made clear to me that I needed to verbalize my sin. The Lord showed me that the tongue is like a dipper reaching down into a well within us and bringing up and out whatever is down there.

Once you clearly ask for the gift of forgiveness, receive it as your own and repeat out loud:

> *Lord, I receive forgiveness for*______________________ (name the sin), *in Christ Jesus. I forgive myself and accept Your gift of forgiveness as my own. I believe that You remove the sin from me completely, putting it at a distance where it can never be found again—as far as the East is from the West. And I believe, Lord, that You remember it no more.*

You will find that speaking aloud is often helpful to you because by doing so you are declaring your stand upon God's Word. The devil cannot read your mind, but he does understand your words. Declare before all the principalities, powers, and rulers of darkness (see Ephesians 6:12) that Christ has set you free and that you intend to walk in that freedom.

When you speak, sound as though you mean it!

If the devil tries to bring that sin to your mind again in the form of guilt and condemnation, repeat your declaration, telling him: "I was forgiven for that sin! It has been taken care of; therefore, I take no care for it." Satan is a legalist, so if you want to, you can even quote the date on which you asked for and received God's promised forgiveness.

Do not just sit and listen to the devil's lies and accusations; learn to talk back to him!

Confess Your Faults to One Another

In James, chapter 5, the way to be healed and restored is made very clear:

> Is anyone among you afflicted (ill-treated, suffering evil)? He should pray. Is anyone glad at heart? He should sing praise [to God].
>
> Is anyone among you sick? He should call in the church elders (the spiritual guides). And they should pray over him, anointing him with oil in the Lord's name.
>
> And the prayer [that is] of faith will save him who is sick, and the Lord will restore him; and if he has committed sins, he will be forgiven.
>
> Confess to one another therefore your faults (your slips, your false steps, your offenses, your sins) and pray [also] for one another, that you may be healed *and* restored [to a spiritual tone of mind and heart]. The earnest (heartfelt, continued) prayer of a righteous man makes tremendous power available [dynamic in its working]. (vv. 13-16)

We are to confess our faults to one another. But this does not mean that every time we sin, we need to confess it to another person. We know that Jesus is our High Priest. We do not have to go to people to receive forgiveness from God. That was the case under the old covenant, but not under the new covenant.

What is the practical application of James 5:16? I believe we not only need to know the Word of God, but how to apply it practically to our daily lives. A person can be bleeding and know that he has a bandage, but if he does not know how to apply the bandage, he can bleed to death. Many people have the Word of God, yet they are "bleeding to death" (living in torment), because they do not know how to apply the Word in everyday situations.

I believe that James 5:16 should be applied in this manner. First, be sure you know that man cannot forgive sin—that is God's job. Yet, man can pronounce and declare God's forgiveness to you. Man can agree with you concerning your forgiveness. Someone can even pray for you to be forgiven (see 1 John 5:16), just as Jesus did when He was on the cross praying for those who had persecuted Him to be forgiven.

When do you need to apply this passage? I believe a time to consider placing James 5:16 into action is when you are being tormented by your past sins. Being poisoned inwardly keeps you from getting well—physically, mentally, spiritually, or emotionally.

Once exposed to the light, things hidden in darkness lose their power. People hide things because of fear. Satan pounds at the mind with thoughts such as: *What will people say if they learn that I was abused? Everyone will think I'm horrible! I'll be rejected*, etc.

In my meetings, numerous people have come to me for prayer, confiding in me, "I have never told this to anyone, but I feel I need to get it out of my system; I was abused." Often they weep uncontrollably. With this weeping, however, often there comes a release that is desperately needed. Hurting people feel safe with me because they know that I was abused also.

Now, *please* understand that I am not saying that everyone needs to admit to being abused and to ask for prayer for healing. If you are suffering from the effects of abuse, be led by the Holy Spirit, not only in deciding whether you need to confess to someone, but also in deciding to whom you should make your confession. The person must be carefully chosen. I suggest a mature Christian you know you can trust. If you are married, and your spouse fits these criteria, consider him or her first.

You should know that often when a spouse finds out about the situation, he or she will respond with anger toward the abuser. Therefore before you make your confession you should be sure that your spouse is Spirit-controlled and willing to follow God's leading and not personal feelings.

Your spouse may ask you some questions that you can easily misunderstand if you are not fully prepared for them. For example, when I told my husband about my father sexually abusing me all those years, he asked me, "Did you ever try to get him to stop?" and "Why didn't you tell anyone?" Keep in mind that your spouse may not fully understand your situation and feelings and may just need some answers. In my case, as soon as I explained to my husband that I was controlled by fear, he understood.

The practice of confessing our faults to one another and receiving prayer is a powerful tool to help break bondages. I had been having trouble with jealousy in a certain area for some time, and I certainly did not want anyone to know about it, so I refused to ask for prayer. Instead, I chose to fight it out alone, and as a result made no progress at all. As God gave me revelation on James 5:16, "Confess to one another therefore your faults," I came to realize that there were a few areas in my life that were maintaining power over me, simply because I was hiding them and was too proud to bring them out in the open.

Fear can cause us to hide things, but pride can do that too. I humbled myself and confessed my problem to my husband, and he prayed for me. After that, I began to experience freedom in that area.

A Word of Caution

Sometimes people relieve themselves of a problem and, in the process, give the problem to someone else. After hearing me teach on the importance of truth, and how hiding things can cause problems, a woman who attended our meetings came to me to confess that she had always disliked me intensely, and had even been gossiping about me. Then she asked me to forgive her, which, of course, I was willing to do. She left excited that she was rid of her problem, but I was left fighting off bad thoughts about her. I wondered what she had been saying about me, to whom she had been talking, if they had believed her, and how long this had been going on.

Balance, wisdom, and love are key words in the Bible. Operating in these qualities will accelerate your progress. A person who is filled with wisdom and love will think a matter through, seek and receive direction from the Lord, and handle the situation in a balanced way.

PART TWO

But Now I Am Free

So if the Son liberates you [makes you free men], then you are really and *unquestionably free.*

JOHN 8:36

15

Forgiving Your Abuser

FOR MANY PEOPLE, forgiving the one who abused them is the most difficult part of emotional healing. It can even be the stumbling block that prevents healing. Those who have been badly wounded by others know that it is much easier to say the word *forgive* than it is to do it.

I have spent a great deal of time studying and praying about this problem, asking the Lord for practical answers to it. I pray that what I have to say to you on this subject will be a fresh approach to a major issue that must be dealt with.

First, let me say that it is not possible to have good emotional health while harboring bitterness, resentment, and unforgiveness. *Harboring unforgiveness is like drinking poison and hoping your enemy will die!* Unforgiveness poisons anyone who holds it, causing him to become bitter. *And it is impossible to be bitter and get better at the same time!*

If you are a victim of abuse, you have a choice to make. You can let each hurt or problem make you bitter or better. The decision is yours.

How can a hurt or problem make you a better person? God does not bring hurts and wounds upon you, but once they are inflicted upon you, He is able to cause them to benefit you if you will trust Him to do so.

God can make miracles out of mistakes!

Satan intends to destroy you, but God can take whatever the devil sends against you and turn it to your good. You must believe that or you will despair. As the psalmist wrote long ago, "[What, what would have become of me] had I not believed that I would see the Lord's goodness in the land of the living!" (Psalm 27:13).

Recently I received a letter from a woman who wrote, "I know God did not cause your abuse, but if you had not been abused, you could not have helped me." She continued, "Please don't feel too badly about it, because God is using your pain to set others free."

Many years ago I had a choice. I could choose to remain bitter, full of hatred and self-pity, resenting the people who had hurt me as well as all those who were able to enjoy nice, normal lives, those who had never been hurt as I was. Or, I could choose to follow God's path, allowing Him to make me a better person because of what I had been through. I thank Him that He gave me grace to choose His way rather than Satan's way.

God's way is forgiveness.

I remember when I first started trying to walk with God. One evening I realized that I could not be full of love and hate at the same time. So I asked the Lord to remove the hate from me that had been there for so long. It seemed as though He reached down inside me and just scooped it out. After that experience, I never hated my father again, but I still resented him, disliked him, and was uncomfortable when I was around him. I wanted to be free from all the sour feelings and bad attitudes inside me, but the "how to" was a big question for me.

As I continued to study and meditate on the Word of God and to fellowship with the Holy Spirit, the Lord taught me many things. I would like to share with you what I have learned in the years of my progression toward complete healing.

Steps to Emotional Healing

First, you must choose God's way of forgiveness. He will not force it on you. If you want to lead a victorious life and enjoy full emotional health, you must believe that God's way is best. Even if you do not understand it, choose to follow it. It works.

Next, learn about God's grace. Grace is the power of the Holy Spirit that comes to us to help us accomplish God's will. James says of God, "But He gives us more and more grace (power of the Holy Spirit, to meet this evil tendency and all others fully). That is why He says, God sets Himself against the proud and haughty, but gives grace [continually] to the lowly (those who are humble enough to receive it)" (James 4:6).[10]

You may choose to forgive, and yet still have to struggle with frustration because you are attempting to forgive in your own strength, when you need the strength of the Lord. The prophet Zechariah tells us that it is "not by might, nor by power, but by My Spirit . . . says the Lord of hosts" (Zechariah 4:6).

It is not necessary for you to be face to face with your abusers in order to benefit by forgiving them in your heart. In fact, even if those who abused you are no longer living, you will still enjoy great freedom if you choose to release their sins against you.

After choosing to forgive, and realizing that you cannot forgive without God's help, pray and release each person who hurt you. Repeat this prayer aloud:

> *I forgive* ____________ (name) *for* ______________ (whatever was done to you). *I choose to walk in Your ways, Lord. I love You, and I turn this situation over to You. I cast my care upon You, and I believe You for my total*

restoration. Help me, Lord; heal me of all the wounds inflicted upon me.

There are many scriptures that tell us that God vindicates (see Isaiah 54:17). God is the One Who recompenses us; He is our reward (see Isaiah 35:4). He is a God of justice, which only He can bring. He alone can repay you for the hurt done to you, and He alone is qualified to deal with your human enemies.

The Bible encourages believers to live at peace with everyone, trusting God to look after them:

> Beloved, never avenge yourselves, but leave the way open for [God's] wrath; for it is written, Vengeance is Mine, I will repay (requite), says the Lord. (Romans 12:19)

> For we know Him Who said, Vengeance is Mine [retribution and the meting out of full justice rest with Me]; I will repay [I will exact the compensation], *says the Lord.* And again, The Lord will judge *and* determine *and* solve *and* settle the cause *and* the cases of His people.
>
> It is a fearful (formidable and terrible) thing to incur the divine penalties *and* be cast into the hands of the living God! (Hebrews 10:30-31)

One of the main truths the Lord spoke to me while I was dealing with the forgiveness issue was this: "*Hurting people hurt people!*"

The majority of abusers were themselves abused in one way or another. Often those who were raised in dysfunctional homes create a dysfunctional atmosphere in their own homes.

When I looked at my own life, I saw the pattern. I had grown up in a dysfunctional home, so I was creating a dysfunctional atmosphere in my own home. I did not know any other way to behave. This realization was a tremendous help to me.

HURTING PEOPLE HURT PEOPLE!

I really do not believe that my father understood what he was doing to me emotionally, nor do I believe that he realized he was causing a problem for me with which I would be dealing most of my life. When I first confronted my father about what he had done to me, he acted as if he felt his actions were normal. He had been abused as a child, and a spirit of incest was motivating him to do what he had seen other family members do.

I was nearly fifty years old before God instructed me to talk to my parents about the abuse I had endured. I did not really want to talk to them about it, but God said it was time to do so. My father showed no regret at that first confrontation, and it seemed clear to me that he was doing what many people do who are not born again—living selfishly, satisfying their own perverted and demon-controlled desires, with no regard for the consequences of their actions. My father was simply determined that he was going to get what he wanted no matter what it did to me or anyone else.

In talking with my parents at that time, I realized that it did not matter that my father was not sorry, it was still important for me to tell him I forgave him. Forgiving him released me to move on.

We should remember what Jesus said as He hung on the cross suffering for things that were not His fault but were the fault of others, including the very ones responsible for His torment. He said, "Father, forgive them, for they know not what they do" (Luke 23:34).

It is easy to judge, but the Bible tells us that "mercy exults victoriously over judgment" (James 2:13). I do not mean that abusers are not accountable for their sins—all of us must be willing to take responsibility for our own wrongdoing. The Lord shared with me that mercy sees the "why" behind the "what." Mercy and compassion do not look just at the wrongdoing; they look beyond to the person doing the wrong to the childhood, the temperament, and the entire life of the individual. We must remember that God hates sin but loves the sinner.

I had so many problems in my personality that it caused many people to judge and reject me. Jesus never rejected me, nor did He judge me. My sin was judged for what it was, but God knew my heart. Sin is sin, and my actions were wrong, no matter what caused them. But God knew that as a woman abused for fifteen years during her childhood, I was acting out major wounds—and He had mercy on me.

Isaiah prophesied of the coming Messiah: "He shall not judge by the sight of His eyes, neither decide by the hearing of His ears" (Isaiah 11:3).

Often in my teaching, I show people a picture of a geode. This rock is hard, ugly, and crusty on the outside, but it is magnificently lined with beautiful blue and amethyst crystals on the inside.

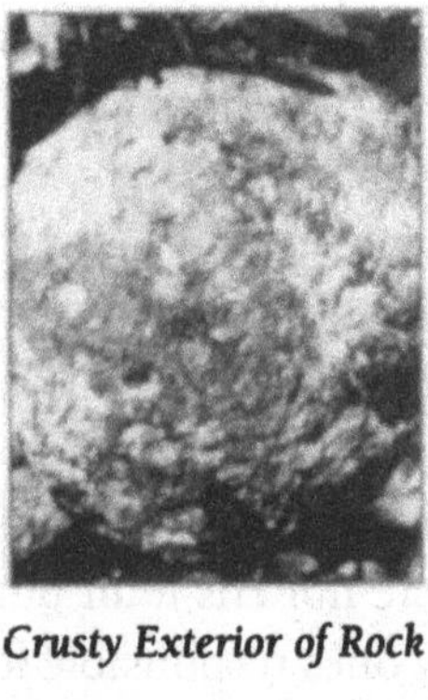

Crusty Exterior of Rock

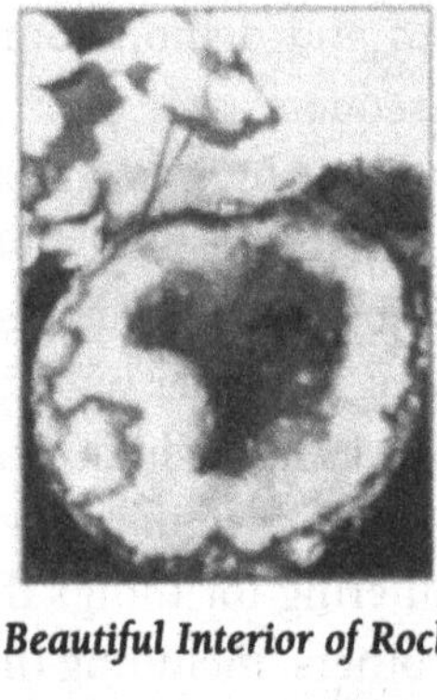

Beautiful Interior of Rock

Looking only at the exterior, who would ever have thought that all that amazing beauty lay just below the surface? That is the way people are. God sees the inside of us. He sees the possibilities. He sees into the spirit. Everyone else sees the outer man. Unless we are trained by God to see beyond what can be perceived with the natural eye, we will always live with judgment in our hearts.

Remember: Hurting people hurt people!

16

Blessing Your Enemies

JESUS WAS QUITE clear about what we are to do to those who hurt us:

> But I tell you, Love your enemies and pray for those who persecute you. (Matthew 5:44)

> Invoke blessings upon *and* pray for the happiness of those who curse you, implore God's blessing (favor) upon those who abuse you [who revile, reproach, disparage, and high-handedly misuse you]. To the one who strikes you on the jaw *or* cheek, offer the other jaw *or* cheek also; and from him who takes away your outer garment, do not withhold your undergarment as well. (Luke 6:28-29)

Paul also instructed believers to forgive others, saying, "Bless those who persecute you [who are cruel in their attitude toward you]; bless and do not curse them" (Romans 12:14).

As I began to minister to people, I noticed that quite often they would express a genuine desire to forgive their enemies but would admit that they were unable to do so. I went to God in prayer seeking answers for them, and He gave me this message: "My people want to forgive, but they are not obeying the scriptures concerning forgiveness." The Lord led me to several passages about praying for and blessing our enemies.

Many people claim to forgive their enemies, but do not or will not pray for those who have hurt them. Praying for those who have wronged us can bring them to a place of repentance and a true realization of the harm they are causing others. Without such prayer, they may remain in deception.

Pray for God to bless your enemies, those who abuse and ridicule and misuse you. You are not praying specifically for their works to be blessed, but rather for them to be blessed as individuals.

It is impossible for anyone to be truly blessed without knowing Jesus. As a victim of abuse, if you are willing to pray for your abusers, you will activate Romans 12:21: "Do not let yourself be overcome by evil, but overcome (master) evil with good."

Ask God to show mercy, not judgment, to your abusers. Remember, if you sow mercy, you will reap mercy (see Galatians 6:7). Blessing and not cursing your enemies is a very important part of the process of forgiveness. One definition of the word *bless* is to "speak well of," and to *curse* means to "speak evil of."

The Tongue and Forgiveness

When you have been mistreated, it is very tempting to talk to other people about what has been done to you. For the purpose of God-ordained counsel, this type of sharing is necessary. To receive healing, comforting prayer, it is also necessary to reveal what you have suffered at the hands of others. But to spread a bad report and ruin a reputation goes against the Word of God. The Bible teaches us not to gossip, slander, or carry tales. The writer of Proverbs 17:9 says, "He who covers *and* forgives an offense seeks love, but he who repeats *or* harps on a matter separates even close friends."

Quite often we exercise faith to receive healing from our hurts and, at the same time, we fail to obey the royal law of love. In Galatians 5:6, the apostle Paul tells us that faith works and is energized by love: "for love covers a multitude of sins" (1 Peter 4:8).

We can have a talk with the Lord about what was done to us. We can even reveal it to those to whom it is needful or necessary for some reason. But if we want to forgive and recover from hurts and wounds, we must not talk loosely about the problem or the person who caused it. The Bible warns us about vain (useless) conversation (see Matthew 12:36). Unless revealing our problem has some godly purpose, we must discipline ourselves to bear it silently, trusting that God will reward us openly for honoring His Word.

I recall the case of a woman whose husband of more than thirty years became involved in an affair with her best friend. He disappeared with the woman, taking the family savings. This was a Christian family, and, of course, the adultery and unfaithfulness were totally unexpected and shocking to everyone.

The devastated wife fell into the trap of talking about what her husband and friend had done to her, which was not an unnatural thing for her to do in the beginning. However, three years later, after she had received a divorce from her husband who had then married her friend, the woman was still not over the pain she had experienced. She married a wonderful man, who was very good to her, and she said that she wanted to forget the past and get on with her life, but she was unable to forgive and press on.

Listening to a set of my teaching tapes on the subject of the mouth and the power of words, she realized that she was not getting well because she was continually talking to anyone who would listen about what had happened to her. Going over and over the details, she was always recalling the painful memories.

God showed me that some people pray for healing and even say, "I forgive those who hurt me," so He begins a work, a healing process. But they will not allow Him to complete His work because they keep re-opening the wound.

When a physical wound begins to heal, a scab forms, but if it is continually picked off, the wound will never heal. It may even become infected and leave a scar. The same holds true with emotional wounds. Talking about the hurt and the person who caused it is equal to picking off a scab. It continually re-opens the wound and causes it to bleed again.

One of the most helpful things God has revealed to me is the fact that forgiveness requires a discipline of the tongue. The flesh always wants to "repeat or harp on a matter," but covering the offense will bring good results.

If you do need to talk about your problem for counseling, prayer, or some other purpose, you can do it in a positive way.

Example: Which sounds more God-like?

> "For fifteen years my father repeatedly abused me sexually. My mother knew about it and did nothing."

— or —

> "For fifteen years my father sexually abused me. God is healing me. I am praying for my father. I realize that he had hurts in his past and was controlled by demonic forces. My

mother knew about what he was doing to me and should have helped me, but she was paralyzed by fear and insecurity. She probably did not know how to face the situation, so she hid from it."

I am sure you agree that the second example sounds more loving. A few well-chosen words can change the entire flavor of a report. Remember, if you want to get better, you cannot be bitter. If there is any bitterness in you, it is highly likely that it will show up in your conversation. The tone of your voice and your choice of words can reveal a lot about you, if you are willing to be honest. In Matthew 12:34, Jesus says that "out of the fullness (the overflow, the superabundance) of the heart the mouth speaks."

If you want to get over a problem, stop talking about it. Your mind affects your mouth, and your mouth affects your mind. It is difficult to stop speaking of a situation until you stop thinking about it. It is also hard to stop thinking about it if you continually talk about it.

Choose to do what you can do, and God will help you do what you cannot do. Do your best, trust God, and He will do the rest.

It may take some time before you can discipline your tongue completely. Start by obeying the "promptings" of the Holy Spirit. If you receive conviction from Him to be quiet, obey and you will receive a bit more freedom each time you do so.

Also be aware that Satan will try to tempt you in this area. He knows the power of words. Words are containers for power! The mouth is a weapon either for Satan or against him. That is why you must choose your words carefully. Satan will even use well-meaning, loving friends to bring up your problem in conversation. Use wisdom and discretion. Do not be caught in a trap that will open up your wound and cause it to start bleeding again.

Trust God to Change Your Feelings

Feelings (emotions) are a major factor in the process of healing and the issue of forgiveness. You can make all of the correct decisions and, for a long time, not feel any different from the way you felt before you decided to be obedient to the Lord. This is where faith is needed to carry you through.

You have done your part and now you are waiting for God to do His. His part is to heal your emotions, to make you feel well and not wounded. Only God has the power to change your feelings toward the person who hurt you. Inner healing can be accomplished only by God, because He, through the power of the Holy Spirit, lives in you (if you are born again), and He alone can heal the inner man.

Why does God make us wait for healing? Waiting is the difficult part. How well we wait reveals whether we have faith in God. According to Hebrews 6:12, the promises of God are inherited through faith and patience. In Galatians 5:5 the apostle Paul states that we must "by faith anticipate *and* wait for the blessing *and* good for which our righteousness *and* right standing with God [our conformity to His will in purpose, thought, and action, causes us] to hope."

We do not have to wait for results when we follow the flesh. However, the natural human way of handling those who hurt us never produces good results. God's way works, but it works on the principle of sowing seed and patiently waiting for the harvest. You sow good seed by obediently following His plan, which is:

- *Receive* God's forgiveness (and love yourself).
- *Choose* to forgive and release those who hurt you.
- *Pray* for your enemies.
- *Bless* those who have hurt you.

- *Believe* that God is healing your emotions.
- *Wait.*

Waiting is where the battle is won in the spiritual realm. Waiting and keeping your eyes on God put pressure on the demonic forces that initiated the problem to begin with, and they have to give back the ground they have gained. As you keep your eyes on God, He forces the enemy off of your territory:

> HE WHO dwells in the secret place of the Most High shall remain stable *and* fixed under the shadow of the Almighty [Whose power no foe can withstand].
>
> I will say of the Lord, He is my Refuge and my Fortress, my God; on Him I lean *and* rely, *and* in Him I [confidently] trust! (Psalm 91:1-2)

As you read the rest of Psalm 91, you will see that it is full of great promises about how the enemy cannot defeat you. The footnote to Psalm 91 in *The Amplified Bible* says, "The rich promises of this whole chapter are dependent upon one's meeting exactly the conditions of these first two verses." In other words, it will be well for those who dwell in the secret place of God and proclaim the Lord to be their Refuge and Fortress, those who trust Him by leaning their entire being on Him.

Here is an account of an experience I went through that will help clarify my point. A friend, someone I loved, trusted, and had helped in many situations, hurt me very severely. Lies were spread about me that caused great trouble and anguish in my life. Judgment and gossip were involved, and the woman who was one of the major initiators of this mess should have known better.

This particular situation was probably the greatest emotional wounding I had ever experienced in my ministry, because it came from a co-laborer in Christ whom I trusted and with whom I worked. I knew I had to forgive her or else my unforgiveness would poison my ministry and me.

I began the six-step process that I have been explaining to you. The first step, choosing to forgive, was not too difficult. Next, I prayed the prayer of forgiveness, which was not hard. The third step, praying for the woman herself, was a bit more difficult. But the fourth step, blessing her and refusing to talk about her, was probably hardest of all.

It actually appeared that she had gotten by with what she had done without any repercussions, while my feelings were in turmoil. I finally progressed to the point that I believed she was deceived by the devil, and that she had actually believed she was being obedient to God when she did what she did to me.

Although I was trying to apply step five, believing for my emotions to be healed, my feelings toward this woman did not change for six months. Step six, waiting on the Lord, was especially difficult for me because I had to be around this woman all the time. She never apologized for her actions or even indicated that she had done anything wrong. Sometimes I hurt so badly that I thought I could not stand it another day!

I would tell God, "I have done my part. I am trusting You to change my feelings." I learned that, for the process to work, you have to stand your ground and not give up!

About six months went by. Sometimes when I saw this woman, I wanted to explode and tell her off! All I could do was keep asking the Lord to help me control myself. I went through various phases of emotions during those six months. At times I could be more understanding than at others.

One Sunday morning during a church service, I knew that God wanted me to go to this woman, hug her, and tell her that I loved her. I can honestly say that my flesh was cringing. I thought, *Oh no, Lord, not that! Surely You will not require me to go to her when she should be coming to me! What if my going to her makes her think that I am admitting I was at fault?*

I wanted the woman to come and apologize to me, and yet, I felt this gentle pressure to go to her. The Holy Spirit was trying to lead me into the blessings that God the Father had stored up for my life. So often the Lord tries to show us what will bless us, and we never receive the blessing because we are too stubborn to just do what He is showing us to do.

Finally I started toward the woman, hating every second of it in my flesh, but wanting to be obedient to the Lord. As I started toward her, she started toward me. Apparently God was speaking to her also.

When we met, I simply hugged her and said, "I love you." She did exactly the same thing, and that was the end of it. She still has never apologized to me, nor even mentioned what happened; however, because of my obedience to His leading, God broke the yoke of bondage. As far as I was concerned, the whole incident was over, at least for the most part. Occasionally I felt a twinge of pain when I would see this woman, or when someone would mention her name, but I was never emotionally tormented by the situation from that day forward.

Are You Willing to Go the Extra Mile?

The time came when God began dealing with me about honoring and blessing my parents. This was difficult for me to do because neither of them had ever showed any regret for the things that had happened to me. I knew that I had to continue doing what was right in God's eyes, even though I did not *feel* like doing so. Remember, forgiveness is not dependent on whether the person being forgiven deserves it. Forgiveness is a choice that is made as an act of obedience to God's Word.

One time when my father was sick and in the hospital, he thought he was going to die, so he asked Dave and me to come and say a prayer over him. We asked him if he wanted to be saved, and he said yes, but when we prayed with him, all he said was, "I just feel dead inside."

He said, "There's just nothing there." He wanted to be saved, but he still was not sorry for what he had done. We had talked about what he had done to me, and now he made the most interesting statement. He said, "I am sorry that what I did hurt you, but I cannot really, truly say that I am sorry I did it."

I could see that my father had not repented, and he could not receive salvation until he was truly repentant. I also could clearly see that repentance is a gift; when a person feels bad about something he has done, that is a gift from God. But my father's heart was so hard that he just could not lay aside his pride and humble himself to confess his sins.

Eventually God led us to move my parents to St. Louis so they could be close to us, and we could take care of them. That was very hard for me to do because I had had a polite, see-you-on-the-holiday relationship with them before that time. I did not have bitterness or resentment in my heart anymore, but I was not going the extra mile to care for their everyday needs.

But moving them was something God specifically put on my heart to do. I do not recommend that anyone else do this just because God told *me* to do it. Obviously, if someone is still in danger of ongoing abuse, I do not believe God would direct him or her to do what I did. But my parents were aging and needed attention that only we could give them.

When God told us to buy them a home, I thought we would just buy an inexpensive house for them, but God said to get them a good house. So we moved them into a nice home that was less than ten minutes away from our own. We bought them furniture, a car, and basically everything they needed.

Again, I must admit that this was not easy for me to do, but I knew that God was telling me to do it. I am not sure what would have happened if I had not been obedient, but I know that God has blessed me specifically in ways that I would not have been blessed if I had not been willing to do what He told me to do. God even blessed our ministry in ways that it would not have been blessed, because I was faithful to do what He asked me to do concerning my parents—even though it was hard. It is important to understand that sometimes God does ask us to do difficult things.

The first three years after my parents had moved near us, I did not see any change in my dad at all. He was not trying to abuse me anymore, but he was still mean, hateful, and bitter, always responding to life with the same bad attitude. His expression would just make me cringe because he looked so miserable. He still did not treat my mother well, but we just kept showing him kindness and love.

We had been doing nice things for my parents for several years before he finally started saying, "Thank you. I appreciate it. You guys are good to us."

I felt that we had done everything we knew to do for my father. Now we just had to wait. The important thing to remember while waiting on God to move in someone's life, or in your own, is to just keep doing what you know is the right thing to do.

Some good advice that I have learned from experience is: *Obey God and do things His way!* It may be hard sometimes, but it is harder to stay in bondage. Always remember this statement: *Even though it hurts to get free, it hurts more to stay in bondage.*

17

Vengeance Is the Lord's

ANY TIME YOU are hurt by another person, there is always the feeling that he owes you something. Likewise, when you hurt someone else, you may have a sense that you need to make it up to him, or pay him back in some way. Unjust treatment, abuse of any kind, leaves an "unpaid debt" in the spirit realm. Such debts are felt in the mind and the emotions. If revengeful feelings from what others owe you, or from what you owe them, become too heavy, or linger in your heart too long, you may even see unhealthy results in your body.

Jesus taught His disciples to pray, "And forgive us our debts, as we also have forgiven (left, remitted, and let go of the debts, and have given up resentment against) our debtors" (Matthew 6:12). He was speaking about asking God to forgive our sins, and He referred to them as "debts." A debt is something that is owed by one person to another. Jesus said that God will forgive us our debts—release them and let them go; act toward us as if we had never owed Him anything.

He also commanded us to behave the same way toward those who are in debt to us. Once again, let me say that this may sound difficult, but it is much more difficult to hate someone and spend your entire life trying to collect a debt that the person can never pay.

The Bible says that God will give us our recompense (see Isaiah 61:7-8 below). I never paid much attention to that scripture until some years ago, while studying in the area of forgiveness and releasing debts. *Recompense* is a key word for anyone who has been hurt. When the Bible says that God will give us our recompense, it basically means that God Himself will pay us back what is owed us!

Memorize these scriptures concerning God's giving us our recompense:

> Instead of your [former] shame you shall have a twofold recompense; instead of dishonor *and* reproach [your people] shall rejoice in their portion. Therefore in their land they shall possess double [what they had forfeited]; everlasting joy shall be theirs.
>
> For I the Lord love justice; I hate robbery *and* wrong with violence *or* a burnt offering. And I will faithfully give them their recompense in truth, and I will make an everlasting covenant *or* league with them. (Isaiah 61:7-8)

We will discuss double blessings again in later chapters. Several other scriptures say that God is a God of recompense and that vengeance is His. Isaiah 49:4 is the one the Holy Spirit used in my life: "Then I said, I have labored in vain, I have spent my strength for nothing and in empty futility; yet surely my right is with the Lord, and my recompense is with my God."

To seek vengeance is to attempt to pay people back for some harm they have caused. The problem is that revenge is always in vain—it does not remove the hurt or restore the damage. It actually causes more pain and damage.

I certainly labored in vain for many years. The word *vain* means "useless." If you labor in vain, your efforts are useless. It will wear you out physically, mentally, and emotionally if you try to pay back all those who hurt you, or all those whom you have hurt.

Many times those you are hating and trying to take vengeance on are out having a good time, not even knowing or caring how you feel. Dear sufferer, this is laboring in vain. As the scripture says, I had spent my strength for nothing; all my effort was futile until I learned to look to God for my recompense.

Recompense is a word similar in meaning to workmen's compensation. If you get hurt on the job while working for God, He repays you. *Recompense* also means reward. According to the Bible, God Himself is our reward (see Genesis 15:1), but He also rewards us by doing special things for us, giving us "joy unspeakable" (1 Peter 1:8 KJV), and the peace "which passeth all understanding" (Philippians 4:7 KJV). God has blessed my life to such a degree that it is often hard to actually believe that it is really me who feels so good and is so blessed.

For a long time I was filled with hatred and resentment. I was bitter, had a chip on my shoulder, and felt sorry for myself. I took out my feelings on everybody, especially those who were trying to love me.

You must remember that what you are full of, you also have to feed on. When you are filled with anger, bitterness, and resentment, not only do you poison other relationships, but you poison yourself as well. What is in your heart will come out in your conversation, in your attitude, even in your body language and voice tone.

If you are full of poisonous thoughts and attitudes, there is no way to keep them from affecting your entire life. Turn the business of debt collecting over to the Lord Himself. He is the only One Who can do the job properly. Align yourself with His ways, and He will collect your debts and repay you for all your past hurts. It really is glorious to watch Him do it.

I Am Willing, But How?

Write down all the debts you owe and all those owed to you. I am speaking of debts in the spiritual realm, not financial debts. Write across all of them, Canceled! Say aloud, "No person owes me anything, and I owe no person anything. I cancel all debts and give them to Jesus. He is now in charge of paying back what is owed."

If you have hurt someone, you can certainly tell that person that you are sorry and ask for forgiveness. Please do not spend your life trying to pay back others for what you have done to them—that is useless. Only God can make it up to them. Here is a practical example.

While I was raising my children, I was still having lots of emotional ups and downs due to abuse in my past. Having been hurt and not yet knowing God's ways of doing things, I ended up hurting my own children. I did a lot of screaming and yelling. I had a bad temper—and no patience whatsoever. I was just plain hard to get along with, and difficult to satisfy.

I laid down many rules for my children. I gave them love and acceptance when they followed my rules, and I got mad when they did not. I was not merciful. I did not realize that I was treating my children the way I had been treated as a child, which is what most people do who have been abused.

As a result of years of living in a war zone, my older son developed some emotional insecurity and personality problems. There always seemed to be a spirit of strife between us, and, in general, we just never got along with each other. Of course, after receiving the baptism of the Holy Spirit and studying the Word of God, I wanted to repair the damage I had done. I wanted to make up to my son for the way I had treated him. You might say that I wanted to pay him back for the hurt I had caused.

Realistically, I did not know how to repair the damage I had done. I apologized, but I did not know what else to do. For a while I fell into the trap of thinking that I should give him everything he wanted; after all, now I was in his debt. My son has a strong personality, and, at that time, he was not walking with the Lord. He learned quickly how to make me feel guilty. He was manipulating and controlling me emotionally, as well as trying to use my new relationship with the Lord to his advantage.

One day as I was attempting to correct him about his behavior, he responded by saying, "Well, I would not be this way if you had treated me right." My reaction was "normal" for me at that time; I retreated to another room to feel bad about myself.

However, this time God showed me something. He said, "Joyce, your son has the same opportunity to overcome his problems that you do. You hurt him because someone had hurt you. You are sorry, and you have repented; there is nothing more that you can do. You cannot spend the rest of your life trying to undo what has already been done. I will help him, if he will let Me."

I knew I was to tell my son what the Lord had told me. I did, and I made a decision that I would stop trying to pay him back. He went through a few rough years, but he finally got more serious with God and started on his own road toward healing and maturity. He is now the director of World Missions for our ministry, and also one of my good friends, as well as my son and co-laborer in Christ.

I really encourage you to examine this area in your life and allow God to recompense you. His reward is great. There is always a time of waiting where the things of God are concerned, but if you will keep doing what you know God is asking you to do, your breakthrough will come. You will make mistakes; when you do, just repent and go on.

When a baby begins to walk, he never does so without falling down many times. He just gets back up and starts again for his destination. Come to Jesus like a little child. He is holding out His arms to you—head in His direction. Even if you fall down often, get up and keep on going.

Before this chapter comes to an end, I would like to reiterate this point: Not only do we fall into the trap of trying to pay back people who have hurt us, but sometimes we take out our hurt on others who actually had nothing to do with causing it.

For years I tried to collect my emotional debts from my husband, just because he was a man, and I was in relationship with him. This is a widespread problem. Some women hate all men because some man hurt them. A boy who is hurt by his mother may grow up and spend the rest of his adult life hating and abusing women. This is a type of debt collecting. Please realize that such behavior does not solve the problem and will never provide an inner sense of satisfaction that the debt is finally taken care of. There is only one way to cancel the debt, and that is God's way.

18

Free to Rejoice with Others

A TRUE INDICATION of emotional healing is evident when one who has been abused can rejoice when others are blessed. In the previous chapters, we discussed the principle taught in Romans 12:14, which says, "Bless those who persecute you [who are cruel in their attitude toward you]; bless and do not curse them." But the Word of God also teaches us to "rejoice with those who rejoice [sharing others' joy], and weep with those who weep [sharing others' grief]" (Romans 12:15).

It is easy for abused people to be envious of those who have never suffered the way they have. But I feel it is important to encourage those who have been abused to rid themselves of envy and jealousy so they can enjoy complete emotional healing.

The Lord brought this need to my attention when I was ministering a word of encouragement to several people in a meeting.

Suddenly, my husband came on the platform because God had put a strong word in his heart that he needed to share. Dave said, "Five or six people just received a personal word from God through Joyce's ministry. But there is a room full of people sitting here who are jealous and thinking, *I wish it had been for me.*"

And he continued, "God plainly spoke to my heart and said to tell you, 'Until you can be happy for other people when they are blessed, you will never have these kind of things happen to you.'" It really affected people to see that they were jealous even over a word of encouragement that God had given somebody else.

We can envy the spiritual gifts another person has. I used to wish I could sing, and so I would listen to people with great voices and think, *I wish I had a voice like that.*

One day God said, "You know, I put that gift in other people for your enjoyment, not for you to resent that they have it and wish that you had it." He said, "I didn't put that gift in them for them; I put it in them for you."

In the same way, the gifts of God that are in me are for other people. My gifts give me responsibility and hard work, but what they give other people is enjoyment. So we are supposed to enjoy each other's gifts, and not be jealous. God put something in me for you, but He also put something in you for me, which really removes our need to be jealous of each other.

I believe that one of the major causes of jealousy is insecurity, which is a lack of knowledge of what it means to be *in* Christ.

The devil lies to us and tells us that other people are better than we are. He successfully deceives us with negative thought patterns such as: *If I could just have what he has*, or, *If I could just be like her*, or, *If only I could do what they can do*. We think that if we were like others, then we would be as "good" as they are. This kind of wrong thinking causes us to become filled with jealousy and envy.

One of the Ten Commandments is, "You shall not covet your neighbor's house, your neighbor's wife, or his manservant, or his maidservant, or his ox, or his donkey, or anything that is your neighbor's" (Exodus 20:17).

To *covet* means "to wish for enviously."[11] *Envy* is defined as "painful or resentful awareness of an advantage enjoyed by another joined with a desire to possess the same advantage."[12] To be *jealous* is to be "intolerant of rivalry;" or "hostile toward a rival or one believed to enjoy an advantage."[13] A jealous person does not even want others to have what he has. In other words, being as good as someone else is not enough to a jealous person. That does not satisfy him; he wants to be better than the other person.

The Old Testament Law stated that a person had to earn God's favor by perfection and by continually offering sacrifices to make up for his imperfection. This was impossible! If people worked and struggled hard enough, they might be able to keep the first nine commandments. But that tenth one—"Thou shall not covet"—they could not keep, because it had to do with the heart and desire of the individual.

To be righteous by the standard of the Law, a person was required to keep all of the Law perfectly. Keeping most of the Law was not sufficient. Therefore, all people were trapped by the commandment against coveting their neighbor's house or his servants or anything else he might have. This one commandment itself speaks loudly and clearly of just how desperately mankind needed a Savior. We human beings had to have help or we could never have hoped to stand clean before God.

Under the new covenant, every person's worth and value is based strictly on being "in Christ" by virtue of believing in Him totally as everything that individual needs. Christ is our

RIGHTeousness. We are made right, not by having what someone else has, but by faith in Jesus. Understanding this truth brings a sense of security and completely eliminates the need to be jealous or envious.

Parts of the Same Body

One of the best examples God has ever given me to get a point across came to me one day while I was teaching on jealousy. Use your imagination and think of this: I have one body, but it is made up of many different parts. Each of the various parts of my physical body is different. Each looks different, serves a different function, and has different capabilities. Some parts are more visible, while some are hidden and rarely ever seen. (In 1 Corinthians 12 the apostle Paul uses this same example by comparing the body of Christ to our physical body.)

My finger gets to wear a ring, and my eye gets the pleasure of seeing the finger wear that ring. However, the eye never gets to wear a ring. Now if the eye were to get jealous and begin to complain, and to want a ring of its own, and if God were to decide to keep the jealous eye happy by granting its request, just think what a mess my body would be!

If you were to take a ring from your finger and attempt to wear it on your eye, you would quickly understand this message. If the eye were wearing a ring, the head would have to be tilted upward in such a way that the eye could no longer give guidance to the rest of the body, because it would be unable to see.

Therefore, point one is that when we are trying to be something God never intended for us to be, it prevents us from fulfilling our God-given function in the body of Christ. Also if the eye were trying to wear a ring, it would be unable to enjoy seeing the ring on the finger, which is the pleasure God intended the eye to have. Remember: The finger gets to wear the ring, but the eye gets to see the ring. The eye was created to enjoy seeing what the rest of the body has been given.

Point two is obvious: When a person is trying to be something he was not intended to be, it prevents him from the enjoyment that would be his if he would take his rightful place in the body and be satisfied with fulfilling the part God designed for him. I personally believe this is one reason so many people who are going to heaven are not enjoying the trip.

As I said, God dropped this example into my heart while I was teaching. He expounded on it by using hands and feet as a further illustration. Think of this: When my feet get new shoes, my hands are so glad that if my feet are not able to get the new shoes on without some help, my hands help my feet into their new shoes!

This is the way the body is supposed to act—no part being jealous or envious of another part. Each part knows that the Lord created it uniquely for a purpose. Each part enjoys the function it has been assigned in the body, realizing that in God's eyes no one part is any better than another.

Having a different function does not make one part inferior to another. Each part is free to enjoy its place and role and to help other parts when needed without any hesitation. The hand does not say to the feet, "Well, if you think I am going to help you get your new shoes on, you have another think coming! Actually, I think I should have shoes also; I am tired of only wearing gloves and rings. I want to have shoes of my own so I will be like you."

No! This is not the way the hands respond when the feet get new shoes and need help putting them on. And this is not the way we should respond when someone we know needs some help. We should be ready to give others all the help we can in order to see them become all they were intended to be and to enjoy all the blessings God desires to pour out upon them.

Ask yourself: "Am I wearing my ring on my eye, or my shoes on my hands?" If you are, no wonder you are miserable and lacking in joy.

In the third chapter of John's gospel, the disciples of John the Baptist came to him and reported that Jesus was beginning to baptize as John had been doing and that now more people were going to Jesus than were coming to John. This message was carried to John in a wrong spirit; it was intended to make him jealous. The disciples who brought the report were obviously insecure and being used by the devil in an attempt to stir up some wrong feelings in John toward Jesus.

John answered, "A man can receive nothing [he can claim nothing, he can take unto himself nothing] except as it has been granted to him from heaven. [A man must be content to receive the gift which is given him from heaven; there is no other source]" (John 3:27).

What John was saying to his disciples was that whatever Jesus was doing, it was because heaven had gifted Him in that way. John knew what God had called him to do, and he knew what Jesus was called to do. He also knew that a person could not go beyond his call and gifting. John was saying to his followers, "Be content." He knew that God had called him to be a forerunner for Jesus, to prepare the way for Him, and that when it was time for Jesus to come to the forefront, he had to become less visible to the people.

Here are John's words to his disciples in reply to their statement regarding the crowds who were flocking to Jesus: "He must increase, but I must decrease. [He must grow more prominent; I must grow less so]" (John 3:30). What a glorious freedom that John enjoyed! It is wonderful to feel so secure in Christ that we do not have to be in competition with anyone.

Freedom from Competition

The apostle Paul wrote, "Let us not become vainglorious *and* self-conceited, competitive *and* challenging *and* provoking *and* irritating to one another, envying *and* being jealous of one another" (Galatians 5:26).

Instead, Paul exhorts us to grow in the Lord until we come to the point that we can "have the personal satisfaction *and* joy of doing something commendable [in itself alone] without [resorting to] boastful comparison" (Galatians 6:4).

Thank God, once we know who we are in Christ, we are set free from the stress of comparison and competition. We know that we have worth and value apart from our works and accomplishments. Therefore we can do our best to glorify God—not to try to be better than someone else.

Quite often people ask my husband or me what it is like for Dave to be married to a woman who does what I am doing. I am the voice on the radio, the face on the television; I am the one who stands on the platform in front of the people; I am the one who is most seen and talked about. In other words, I am the focal point of our ministry. Dave is the administrator, an important function, but a background position. His work is behind the scenes, not out front as mine is.

Our situation is unique in that it is usually the other way around. Generally, in a team effort, it is the man who occupies the focal position, while his wife works behind the scenes to help him. My husband happens to be secure enough that his sense of worth or value is not affected by what he does or does not do. In fact, he is so secure that (in obedience to the Lord) he has been able to help me be all that I can be in Christ. He is content to help me fulfill the call of God on my life, and, in the process, is fulfilling God's claim on his own life.

Dave's call and his position are certainly just as important as mine. They are just not as noticeable by the public. As administrator for the ministry, he oversees the finances, locates and contracts with radio and television stations interested in carrying our *Life In The Word* broadcast, carefully watches over all the stations that already carry our broadcast to make sure they are bearing good fruit, and handles all of our travel arrangements.

At our meetings, Dave loves working behind the table where our teaching tapes are displayed, talking with the people, and ministering to them. I have asked him numerous times to share the platform with me, and his reply has always been the same, "That is not where I am supposed to be. I know my place, and I am going to stay in it." That is the statement of a mature, secure man.

People have a tendency to ask Dave, "Are you Joyce's husband?" He usually replies, "No, Joyce is my wife."

Dave fulfills many, many important functions in our ministry, but in summing up his role, he usually says, "I am called by God to be Joyce's covering, to get her where God wants her to be. I make sure she does not get hurt, and I see to it that she does not get in trouble."

Sometimes there are things I want to do that Dave will not allow because he feels that they are unwise or that the timing is wrong. I will not say that it is always easy to submit to his desires if they are not mine, but I have learned that his gifts bring balance to our lives and our shared ministry.

Dave wrestled with our situation for a couple of years in the beginning. Actually, he did not want to be in ministry at all. However, God showed him that He had given me the gift of teaching His Word. Dave says, "God did not ask me to submit to my wife, but He did ask me to submit to the gift He put in her." He says that God showed him that the gift was His and that by submitting to that gift and allowing me to do what He had called me to do, Dave was submitting to the Lord Himself.

Dave not only allows me to do what God has called me to

do, he helps me do it. I consider it a great honor to be married to Dave Meyer. As far as I am concerned, he is the greatest man I know. He is also the happiest, most contented person I know.

When I say that Dave is always happy, I mean it literally. He enjoys life to the fullest. I believe, and so does Dave, that this joy is a result of his submitting to God and not trying to become something that the Lord has not called him to be. He is not in competition with anyone. He is not trying to prove anything to anyone.

SECURELY ROOTED AND GROUNDED

My prayer from the beginning of this book has been for you to be "rooted deep in love *and* founded securely on love, that you may have the power *and* be strong to apprehend *and* grasp with all the saints [God's devoted people, the experience of that love] what is the breadth and length and height and depth [of it]" (Ephesians 3:17-18).

When we are free from the need to compete with other people, we are free to help them succeed. When we really know who we are, we do not have to spend our lives trying to prove our worth and value to ourselves or to others.

Dave knows he is important to God, and so, what the world thinks of his position as compared to mine does not concern him at all. I believe that Dave's decision and life can be a testimony to many. There is much to be done in the kingdom of God, and it will best be accomplished if all of us work together in whatever individual capacity God assigns us.

Let us all lay aside jealousy, envy, competition, and comparison. Remember, these problems are rooted in insecurity. The good news is that we can be free from insecurity and, therefore, free from the problems it causes. Isaiah 54:17 says in part: "This [peace, righteousness, security, triumph over opposition] is the heritage of the servants of the Lord." That means that part of our inheritance as sons and daughters of God is security! Start spending your inheritance now.

Rejoice for others and enjoy the contentment, satisfaction, peace, and joy that come from knowing that God loves you and views you as righteous and valuable through your faith in His Son Jesus Christ. Be firmly rooted in and securely grounded on His love for you.

19

Emotional Stability

EARLIER IN THE book I mentioned the term "addictive behaviors" to describe the types of behavior that can develop when a person has been abused and has a shame-based nature. In this section, I would like to deal specifically with what I call "emotional addictions" and how to break them in order to enjoy emotional stability.

In this context, an *addiction* can be defined as compulsory behavior, often in response to some stimulus, without conscious thought. People who have been hurt tend to react rather than to act. What I mean is that they tend to react out of their wounded emotions, rather than to act according to wisdom and the Word of God.

For many years, whenever I was faced with a situation or a personality that reminded me of the past, I responded emotionally, reacting out of fear instead of acting on faith. These types of incidents can be very confusing to the wounded victim because everything happens so quickly that he really does not even understand why he is behaving as he is.

For example, the person who abused me had a very strong,

domineering personality. I was subjected to a lot of manipulation and control during my childhood. I decided and repeatedly promised myself that when I was old enough to leave home and get out on my own, nobody would ever control me again.

In subsequent years, I had a warped view of authority. I saw all authority figures as my enemy. I was so fearful of being controlled and manipulated that when any person in my life tried to get me to do anything I did not want to do, I would react with rage or withdrawal. Often the incidents were very minor. Even a suggestion from someone that was not in line with my wishes could cause me to act strangely. I had no more understanding of my actions than anyone else. Logically, I knew I was behaving badly; I did not want to act that way, but I seemed powerless to change.

God began to teach me about emotional addictions, showing me that in the same way that people can become addicted to certain chemical substances in their physical bodies (i.e., drugs, alcohol, nicotine, caffeine, sugar), they can also develop mental and emotional addictions. Remember, an *addiction* is compulsory behavior done without thinking it through. My violent reactions were basically my way of saying to others, "You are not going to control me!"

I was so fearful of being controlled that I overreacted to every situation, trying to protect myself when there was no real problem. The rage said, "I will not let you control me!" And the withdrawal said, "I refuse to get involved with you!" A person cannot get hurt if he refuses to get involved. Therefore, whenever anything painful occurred in any of my relationships, I either attacked it or refused to deal with it at all. Both of these types of behavior are out of balance and unscriptural; they only increase the problem of addiction by feeding it.

If a person is addicted to drugs, then the more drugs he

takes, the more he is likely to need. The longer he allows his addiction to control him, the more it demands from him. Eventually it will consume him. The addiction must be broken. And that means denying the flesh the substance it is accustomed to, and going through the pain of withdrawal in order to get free of it. The same principle applies to mental or emotional addictions.

Addicted to Worry and Reasoning

One of my mental addictions was worry. I worried and worried and worried. Even when there was nothing to worry about, I found something. I developed a false sense of responsibility, always attempting to solve problems for which I had no responsibility or solution. I reasoned, figured, and lived in constant confusion.

As a result, my mind was continually filled with worry and reasoning. Although it made me physically and mentally exhausted and stole any hint of joy in my life, I could not seem to control it. Worry and reasoning were my automatic responses to any problem. Although my behavior was abnormal, it was normal for me because that was the way I had always reacted to problems.

The Word of God says, "Trust (lean on, rely on, and be confident) in the Lord" (Psalm 37:3). However, trust is not an easy thing if you have been abused. The people you trusted to take care of you did not do it; instead, they used you. They hurt you terribly, so you made a promise to yourself that nobody would ever hurt you again. You do not wait to discover whether others will hurt you or not; you simply put up walls of protection around yourself to shield yourself from harm.

One of the ways you protect yourself is by trying to figure out everything. If you can accomplish this, you think you have everything under control, and there are no surprises to upset you.

When God began to work in my life, He showed me clearly that I was addicted to worry and reasoning, and that I had to give them up. If there was a problem in my life, and I was not trying to solve it, then I felt totally out of control inside. You must remember that I wanted to be in complete control of everything that was going on around me—that way I thought I would not get hurt.

I believed that I would take good care of myself, but I did not believe that anyone else would take care of me.

Deny Yourself

Jesus said, "If anyone intends to come after Me, let him deny himself [forget, ignore, disown, and lose sight of himself and his own interests] and . . . follow with Me [continually, cleaving steadfastly to Me]" (Mark 8:34).

As the Lord continued to work with me in His patient ways, He taught me that I could trust Him, and that I could believe He was working on my problem even when I was not. My part was to step out in faith and refuse to worry or reason. I had to deny my mind the addictive behavior it was accustomed to; as I did so, eventually I was set totally free from it.

I did have some withdrawal symptoms—feeling afraid, out of control, and even stupid, at times. (The devil will try anything to keep a person in bondage—even making him feel ridiculous.)

In Mark 8:34 Jesus teaches us that in order to follow Him, we must deny ourselves, and our way, and choose His way. My way was to take care of myself. His way for us is to deposit ourselves with Him and learn by experience that He will never fail us or forsake us (see Hebrews 13:5). In order to learn this truth, I had to first give up my way.

Like a Weaned Child

The psalmist must have been aware of the same things we are discussing in this chapter on breaking addictions when he wrote: "Surely I have calmed and quieted my soul; like a weaned child with his mother, like a weaned child is my soul within me [ceased from fretting]" (Psalm 131:2). He even mentions his soul being weaned.

The soul is often defined as the mind, will, and emotions. We see from this scripture that these areas may become addicted to certain types of behavior just as the body may become addicted to certain types of substances.

By denying my mind the privilege of worrying and reasoning, I was weaned from my mental addiction just as a baby is weaned from its bottle or pacifier. And even as the baby has fits of crying and trying all sorts of ways to get the bottle or pacifier back, I also had fits of anger, crying, and self-pity. I even had occasional attacks of fear, but I continued to conform myself to God's way until I was totally delivered from following my way.

Jesus said that He came to release the captives (see Luke 4:18), and that he whom the Son has set free is free indeed (see John 8:36 KJV).

20

Intimacy and Trust

FOR A PERSON who has been abused, intimacy is often very difficult. Intimacy requires trust, and once the trust factor has been destroyed, it must be restored before intimacy will be comfortable.

Since people always hurt people, we cannot depend on others never to hurt us. I cannot tell you, "Just trust people; they won't hurt you." They may not intend to hurt you, but we may as well face the reality that people hurt people.

As I have already mentioned, my husband is a wonderful, kind, easygoing man; yet, there are times when he hurts me, just as there are times when I hurt him. Even people who love each other very much sometimes hurt and disappoint each other.

It took many years before I was comfortable being intimate with my husband and could honestly say that I enjoyed our sex life. I was so fearful of being hurt and taken advantage of that I could not relax. My basic attitude was, "If we must do this, then let's just get it over with, so I can forget it and go on to something else." Of course, my husband could sense my attitude, even though I tried to hide my true feelings and pretend that I enjoyed our sexual relationship.

My attitude made Dave feel rejected. Had he not been a mature Christian who had some discernment from the Lord about what was going on in me, my attitude could have done severe damage to his concept of himself as a man, let alone as a husband. He once said to me, "If I were depending on you to tell me what kind of a man I am, I would be in serious trouble."

I am grateful that the Lord gave me a mature Christian man for my husband. I am grateful that I did not destroy him while I was being healed. So often, troubled people marry troubled people. After they have destroyed each other, their problems are transferred to their children, who in turn become the next generation of troubled, tormented people.

For many years I evaded the issue. Deep down inside I knew that I needed to deal with my attitude regarding sex and intimacy, but I continued to put it off month after month, year after year. Do you have a tendency to put off things that God is trying to get you to deal with? We do that because some issues are too painful even to think about, much less go through.

Finally, I made the decision to stop procrastinating and to face the truth. In this situation the truth was as follows: (1) I had a problem, but I was punishing Dave for it. (2) He had been very patient with me, but it was time for me to deal with my problem. (3) As long as I continued to behave as I did, the devil would continue to defeat me because I was allowing my past to affect my present and my future. (4) Putting off dealing with the problem would be nothing more than direct disobedience to the Holy Spirit.

Of course, I was very much afraid; I did not even know how to begin. I remember crying out to God, "But how can You expect me to trust Dave? What if he takes advantage of me? Or what if . . ." The devil never runs out of "what ifs."

I specifically remember the Lord saying to me, "I am not asking you to trust Dave; I am asking you to trust *Me*." This put a totally different perspective on the situation. It was easier for me to trust God than people, so that is where I started.

I simply committed to do whatever the Lord showed me in my heart I was to do and to trust Him with my feelings about it. For example: I always wanted the lights out while Dave and I made love. I recall that in my heart I came to realize that I should leave them on, and so I did. That was difficult, but once I did it a few times, it got easier and easier. Now I am free to leave the lights on or turn them off; it does not matter anymore because I am not hiding from anything.

Another example: I never would approach Dave to show any interest in having sex with him. There were times when I desired him; my physical body had a need, but I would not approach him. I began to realize that when I felt that I wanted him, I needed to take some action to let him know. This was particularly difficult for me because I always felt that sex was wrong or dirty, because that was the way it had been initially presented to me in my childhood.

My first sexual experiences were perverted, so my attitude toward sex was perverted. Mentally, I knew that sex was originally God's idea, but I could not seem to get past my feelings. Once again, taking "obedient action" broke the bondage, and now I am free in this area also.

Please understand that when the Holy Spirit is prompting you to do something, He is doing it to help you, to bless you, and to set you free in some way. *The Holy Spirit is the Helper and only has your good in mind.* People may hurt you, but God will not. Some of the things He leads you through may hurt for a while, but God ultimately will work them for your good.

As I continued this process of choosing to do what the Lord

was showing me, I enjoyed progressive freedom, and so will you. There were many instances too numerous to mention here, but I think you understand what I am talking about. You will have your own situations to face, and the Holy Spirit will walk you through your healing process concerning intimacy and trust.

Refuse to live the rest of your life in a prison of suspicion and fear!

Trust the Lord

I know I have said this in other places in this book, but I feel prompted to say it again. The main thing that helped me in this area of trust, as well as in other areas, was simply to realize that God is not asking us to put our trust in people, but in Him.

We can also learn to trust people in a balanced way. If we get out of balance, we will get hurt. Often, God uses these situations to teach us the wisdom of keeping relationships in balance.

In dealing with this issue, I often look to Jeremiah 17:

> Thus says the Lord: Cursed [with great evil] is the strong man who trusts in *and* relies on frail man, making weak [human] flesh his arm, and whose mind *and* heart turn aside from the Lord. For he shall be like a shrub *or* a person naked and destitute in the desert; and he shall not see any good come, but shall dwell in the parched places in the wilderness, in an uninhabited salt land. (vv. 5-6)

Think about these verses. They say bluntly that we are going to find curses (trouble) if we give man the trust that rightfully belongs to the Lord. The arm of the flesh mentioned here can be referring to trusting self as well as trusting others.

When I look to myself to meet my needs, I fail; and when I look to others to meet my needs, they fail me. The Lord requires that He be allowed to meet our needs. When we look to the Lord, He often uses people to meet our needs, but we are looking to and depending on Him—not the people through whom He works—and this is the balance He requires of us.

And now the good news: "[Most] blessed is the man who believes in, trusts in, *and* relies on the Lord, and whose hope *and* confidence the Lord is. (v. 7)"

There were times in the past when I would feel discouraged and get angry at the people around me because they were not giving me the encouragement I needed. As a result, I would have a resentful attitude of self-pity that my family and others could not understand. It certainly did not result in having my needs met because I was looking to people when I should have been looking to God.

The Lord taught me that when I needed encouragement, I should ask Him for it. As I learned to do that, I discovered that He would provide the needed encouragement through the source He chose. I learned that it was not necessary for me to put pressure on relationships in an effort to get from people what only God could give me. The next verse in this passage announces the hope that we have if we put our trust in God:

> For he shall be like a tree planted by the waters that spreads out its roots by the river; and it shall not see *and* fear when heat comes; but its leaf shall be green. It shall not be anxious *and* full of care in the year of drought, nor shall it cease yielding fruit. (v. 8)

This verse assures us that as we place our trust in God instead of the frail arm of the flesh, we will become *stable.* I emphasize this word because it is very important to our discussion. There can never be any real enjoyment in life without a sense of stability.

Let these verses encourage you to place your trust in God and not in people. *Do not look to others to meet your needs; look to God. Anything people may do to you, God can fix.*

One final thought concerning intimacy. God has created all of us to thoroughly enjoy one another. In particular, the Bible says that a husband and wife should enjoy each other, as written in Proverbs 5:18, "Let your fountain [of human life] be blessed [with the rewards of fidelity], and rejoice in the wife of your youth."

Part of enjoying your spouse and your marriage is enjoying intimacy. Take a step of faith and realize that fear of being hurt is hurting you more than facing that fear and finding freedom. Trust God with the people in your life. You may not be able to handle them, but He is able.

THE IMPORTANCE OF BALANCE IN RELATIONSHIPS

Ask yourself if you have any relationships that are out of balance. Is there anyone in your life on whom you are depending too much? When you have problems, do you run to the throne or the phone? Are you looking to people to keep you happy, or are you looking to the Lord?

I recall a time when I was attacked by fear that something might happen to my husband. I began thinking, *What would I do if Dave died?* It was a panic-filled type of thinking, which was unusual for me. I had never even considered what I would do if Dave should die before I did. Like most women who have good marriages, I depend on my husband a lot. Dave is good to me, and as I thought of all the things he does for me, I became more and more panic-stricken.

Then the Lord spoke this to me in the depths of my heart: "Joyce, if Dave died, you would keep on doing exactly what you are doing. It is not Dave who is upholding you and causing you to do what you are doing, it is Me; so put your trust in Me, where it belongs. Trust Dave, but do not get out of balance."

One final example I would like to share with you concerns a certain friendship and working relationship in my life. Sexual intimacy is not the only kind of intimacy that needs to be restored to wounded people. Those who have been abused often experience difficulty in maintaining any type of relationship. Their marriage relationship is affected, and Satan also seeks to use their hurts and disappointments to ruin *all* their close relationships.

Like many others in the world, not only was I abused in my early years at home, but even after I had gotten away from that situation, I continued to be easily hurt by nearly everyone I encountered. When I finally got married and joined the church, I thought that surely church people would not hurt me. I soon discovered, however, that the pain did not stop just because I was a church member. In fact, in some instances, it became more severe. The result for me was that I did not trust men because it was a man who had hurt me, which affected my marital intimacy. I had also been hurt severely by friends and relatives at various times, so I honestly was afraid to trust anyone.

As the years went by and Dave and I got involved in full-time ministry, a couple came to work for us who were definitely sent by the Lord. They were anointed by God to be "armor-bearers" for us. That means that they prayed for us regularly; they worked side by side with us, and were available to do whatever needed to be done, whenever it needed to be done. They were very good to us, and they made our lives a lot easier.

The scope of our ministry would have been much different if we had not had this wonderful couple, or someone like them, to help us. Because of the years of hurt I had experienced, I did not open my heart too readily, but as time passed, I came to trust these people very much and to depend on them quite heavily.

One day I read the scripture in which the psalmist said, "Even my own familiar friend, in whom I trusted (relied on and was confident), who ate of my bread, has lifted up his heel against me" (Psalm 41:9). I knew that verse applied to me and began to wonder who the Lord was warning me about. I knew He was trying to show me something, because I kept supernaturally coming across the same scripture repeatedly. I was convinced that God was saying something. I began to wonder if He was showing me that it was this couple who was going to hurt me.

Finally, the Lord made Himself clear enough for me to understand that He was just warning me not to let our relationship get out of balance. He taught me that we could have a close relationship, enjoy years of faithful, loyal service, and produce a lot of good fruit for His kingdom. But I was being specifically warned not to put a trust in them that belongs only to Him. He let me know that He had brought that couple into my life, and He could certainly take them away, which He would do if I put my eyes on them as my source of help instead of keeping my trust in Him.

Even intimacy in a good friendship is scriptural, but it must not get out of balance. Think of David and Jonathan. The Bible says, "The soul of Jonathan was knit with the soul of David, and Jonathan loved him as his own life" (1 Samuel 18:1). They helped each other and enjoyed covenant relationship. Good friendship is very important, but so is balance.

I stress the importance of balance because the apostle Peter says, "Be well balanced . . . for that enemy of yours, the devil, roams around like a lion roaring [in fierce hunger], seeking someone to seize upon *and* devour" (1 Peter 5:8). Stay in balance, and the devil will not be able to devour you or your relationship with others.

21

Ask and Receive

THE BIBLE SAYS in James 4:2, "You do not have, because you do not ask." I remember when that was a great revelation in my life because I was trying to make things happen in the energy of my own flesh, according to my own plan, and as the result of my own works. I was trying to change myself, trying to change my husband, trying to change my circumstances, trying to rid myself of all the things from my past that were hurting me. But I was not asking God for help.

When God revealed to me that I was lacking good things because I was not asking of Him, I began to ask Him for everything I desired and needed.

The Word says, "Delight yourself also in the Lord, and He will give you the desires *and* secret petitions of your heart" (Psalm 37:4). God began doing more for me as a result of my asking, proving to me that He wanted to take care of me. He showed me that if I would ask Him, just come to Him like a little child and ask Him, then *He* would do for me, *He* would take care of me, *He* would meet my needs.

I believe that you may be reading this book because you

hope to get a breakthrough of healing from your wounded past. You may need for God to heal your broken heart. You may be tired of being all messed up and frustrated inside, as I was. You may need to ask God for help. If so, simply pray:

Lord, heal me. I am asking You for a breakthrough. Give me an answer. Show me the direction I need to go. Help me, Lord.

Ask in Jesus' Name

I believe that there may be an issue that must be settled in your heart before you can believe that God will meet your needs. An important key concerning your breakthrough is found in John 16:24. Jesus was talking to His disciples just before His crucifixion when He said, "Up to this time you have not asked a [single] thing in My Name [as presenting all that I AM]; but now ask *and* keep on asking and you will receive, so that your joy (gladness, delight) may be full *and* complete."

The Amplified Bible tells us what it means to ask in the name of Jesus. If you can grasp what it means to ask in Jesus' name, it will give you a breakthrough to the miracle you need.

To ask in Jesus' name means to present to the Father all that Jesus is. Therefore, when we go before the throne, we are not presenting who we are, but the authority Jesus has because of His covenant relationship with the Father.

We are not presenting our own record of good works. We have no perfection to present. But we go before the Father and say, "Lord, I come in the name of Jesus." When we say that, we are really saying to the Father, "I am presenting to You what Jesus is."

When you go somewhere in somebody's name, you go with that person's authority. For example, I am very close to our pastor in St. Louis. I consider him to be a good friend of ours. I could go to his office and say to his staff, "It is important that I see the pastor right away." His staff know me and trust me well enough to let me in right away.

But if I could not go myself, I might send someone who was not known at the pastor's office. If that person said simply, "I need to see the pastor *now*," the pastor's staff probably would not let him in right away. But if he said, "Joyce Meyer sent me," the staff would receive him in my name because of the relationship *I* have with the pastor.

That is a picture of what it means to pray in Jesus' name; that is why you can expect to have your needs met when you go to God the Father in the name of His Son—not because you deserve it. If there is anything I am trying to teach you in these few pages, it is that we do not *deserve* anything from God, except maybe to die and be punished eternally. But He has made a new covenant with us to give us what Jesus deserves. That undeserved covenant blessing is the glory of the message of grace.

We do not deserve anything, but we get what Jesus earned and deserved. And it is free! *Free* is an exciting word. We do not have to try to earn blessings with our good works or good behavior. In John 16:24 (paraphrased) Jesus said, "Up until now you have not asked a single thing *in My name* (that is, presenting all that I am)." In that same verse, He gave us a new instruction. "But now," He said, "ask, and you will *receive, so* that your joy may be full." Jesus gave two instructions here: "Do not just ask, but ask *and receive*, so that your joy may be full."

Receive God's Blessings

Many people simply do not know how to receive from God. For example, they spend half of their life begging God to forgive them for some sin, but they never *receive* His forgiveness. They just stay in the begging mode. I asked for forgiveness for years, every night, in fact.

When Dave and I were first married, I did not know much of the Word of God. We were going to church; I loved God; I was born again; but I certainly did not know who I was in Christ, and I still had a broken heart. I believe one of the things that refers to being brokenhearted is to be broken in personality.

Our personalities get shattered and broken, and then we do not function the way God intends for us to function. Every person is to be a whole and balanced individual. But the devil wants to work us over to the point that we are all broken in personality. When that happens, we may try to relate to each other, but our relationships just do not work.

As mentioned earlier, I used to kneel at my bedside every night and beg, "Oh, God, forgive me. God, forgive me. God, forgive me." Every night, I repeated that prayer: "God, forgive me. Oh, God, forgive me." I was still talking about that load of guilt I had been carrying since my teenage and young adult years.

This went on and on for a couple of years, until the day I heard the Lord say to me, "Joyce, I forgave you the first time you asked Me. Now you need to forgive yourself." Hearing God's voice was not a common occurrence for me in those days, but I understood that He was telling me that I needed to *receive* His forgiveness.

If you ask someone for a drink of water, and that person gives it to you, but you refuse to swallow it, what can that individual do about it? It would be senseless to say, "I am thirsty; somebody bring me some water because I am *so* thirsty," and then just hold the glass of water you are given. If you would not swallow it, your thirst would not be quenched.

You may have been given the Word about forgiveness, but you may not have decided yet to believe it. You may be waiting to *feel* forgiven first. But you will never *feel* forgiven until you decide that you *are* forgiven. You have to say in faith, "I am forgiven." And you may have to say it for weeks or months before your feelings catch up with your faith.

Throughout the Bible we are instructed to *receive* from God. But it seems that Christians are always trying to *get* something. Paul did not ask the disciples at Corinth, "Did you *get* the Holy Spirit?" He asked them, "Did you *receive* the Holy Spirit when you believed [on Jesus as the Christ]?" (Acts 19:2).

The Bible does not say, "To as many as *get* Jesus, they get the power to become sons of God." It says, "But as many as *received* him, to them *gave he* power to become the sons of God, even to them that believe on his name" (John 1:12 KJV, emphasis mine).

Jesus is like a River of Life that is pouring out life-giving water, and we are invited to receive, receive, and receive. Jesus said:

> He who believes in Me [who cleaves to *and* trusts in *and* relies on Me] as the Scripture has said, From his innermost being shall flow [continuously] springs *and* rivers of living water. But He was speaking here of the Spirit, Whom those who believed (trusted, had faith) in Him were afterward to *receive*. For the [Holy] Spirit had not yet been given, because Jesus was not yet glorified (raised to honor). (John 7:38-39)

I have taught extensively on this subject of receiving from God, because I am so convinced that people are not receiving the blessings that God wants to impart to them. I am eager to see everyone in the body of Christ become mature and say, "Yes, that promise of God is for me, and I receive it so that I do not have to live under guilt and condemnation anymore."

God Loves You Perfectly

I can talk about the love of God throughout an entire weekend conference, I can demonstrate all the different ways that God has proven His love for us, but I cannot force anyone to receive His love. It is a personal choice that each person has to make. Even when we make mistakes and know that we do not deserve the love of God, we must still *receive* His love in order to enjoy the fullness of what He wants us to have.

I encourage you to practice on a daily basis opening your mouth and praying:

God, I know that You love me, and I receive that love; I am going to walk in it today. I am going to bask in Your love, because I know that You love me even though I do not deserve it. And God, that makes everything better.

The love of God is one of the most relevant messages needed in the body of Christ today. God's love is the greatest issue in which people need to have a revelation. People do not need a teaching about the love of God as much as they need to personally experience and understand how much God loves them as an individual.

The love of God will carry you through to victory when all of the powers and principalities of hell seem to be against you. The love of God will carry you through the storms of life and into a place of calm peace. But you will never be more than a conqueror (see Romans 8:37) if you do not have a revelation of how much you are loved by God.

We have to know that God loves us even during the times when we make mistakes and fail. His love is not restricted to the days when we think we have performed well. We need to be confident of His love especially when we have trials, and when the devil is mocking us with accusations, such as, "Well, you must have done something wrong."

When the accuser comes, we must know that God loves us.

Even if we did do something wrong, even if we did open a door for the devil to enter in, even if we did act in ignorance, God still loves us. God is on our side (see Romans 8:28), and He is going to show us what we need to do to get out of the mess we got ourselves into. But Satan wants to cut us off from the love of God, so that we never find the way back to God's grace in order to live as His RIGHTeous sons and daughters.

Jesus Sends His Word

When we are in trouble, the Lord promises in His Word to deliver us. It is written in Psalm 107:20, "He sends forth His word and heals them and rescues them from the pit *and* destruction." Jesus sent His Holy Spirit to teach us what we need to know. He said to His disciples:

> I have still many things to say to you, but you are not able to bear them *or* to take them upon you *or* to grasp them now.
>
> But when He, the Spirit of Truth (the Truth-giving Spirit) comes, He will guide you into all the Truth (the whole, full Truth). For He will not speak His own message [on His own authority]; but He will tell whatever He hears [from the Fa-

> ther; He will give the message that has been given to Him], and He will announce *and* declare to you the things that are to come [that will happen in the future].
>
> He will honor *and* glorify Me, because He will take of (receive, draw upon) what is Mine and will reveal (declare, disclose, transmit) it to you.
>
> Everything that the Father has is Mine. That is what I meant when I said that He [the Spirit] will take the things that are Mine and will reveal (declare, disclose, transmit) it to you. (John 16:12-15)

I am so glad Jesus promises that the Holy Spirit will *guide* us—not *push* and *shove* us, but guide us—to truth. The devil wants to pressure us and manipulate us, but the Holy Spirit wants to gently lead us. That is one of the ways that we can recognize whether we are hearing from God or from the enemy.

If you feel pressed, confused, controlled, or stressed about something, then it is not of God; that is not how He works. Instead, the Holy Spirit will gently "reveal, (declare, disclose and transmit)" the truth to you.

But, revelation will not benefit you if you do not receive it. We have transmissions through television, but we have to turn our set on in order to *receive* the messages sent to us. Likewise, we must receive the truth that God is speaking to us through His Word.

Jesus won everything that we would ever need to live victorious, overcoming, power-packed lives. When Jesus ascended on High, the Holy Spirit took what Jesus had earned and in essence said, "Now, I will go to the believers and work with them, ministering to them everything that Jesus has earned and provided for them. I will lead and guide them into all the truth."

It is interesting that Jesus said there was so much more He

wanted to tell us, but He knew we could not bear it all at once. But He promised that the Holy Spirit would take what is His and *guide* us into all truth.

Receive the Holy Spirit

I was born again a long time before I enjoyed the presence of the Holy Spirit in my life. I loved God, and I would have gone to heaven if I had died; but I would have arrived there a wreck. Without the fellowship of the Holy Spirit, I would have never been a fruit-bearing Christian.

My life would have never glorified God here on the earth. I would have never been a witness to anybody else. As a matter of fact, if I had not *received* the Holy Spirit, claiming to be a Christian could have actually been a detriment to the work of God in my life because I was not acting like I was a Christian.

I was out of control, and I could not help it. I did everything that I believed a good Christian was supposed to do, but I had no victory because I did not have any knowledge of the Word of God. And I did not have the power of the Holy Spirit to guide me into truth or to reveal how that Word was to work in my life.

It was a glorious day when I first said out of my mouth, "I am the righteousness of God in Jesus Christ" (see 1 Corinthians 1:30). I felt my spirit do a flip; I literally felt life leap inside of me. I remember thinking, *What was that?* It was like the feeling a mother has when a baby moves within her for the first time—only, it was the Holy Ghost!

Before I received the Holy Spirit, I did not know that I was righteous. I thought I was rotten, no good, and messed up for life. I felt that there was no hope for me, and that is what the devil wants us all to believe, but it is a lie.

If you would like to learn more about the fellowship of the Holy Spirit, I encourage you to read my book *Knowing God Intimately*. In it, I explain how you can be as close as you want to be to God, and how to receive the fullness of the Holy Spirit into your life. It is really as simple as praying, *Lord, I receive Your Holy Spirit into my life. Fill me with Your presence, and teach me to clearly hear Your voice so that I may follow You all the days of my life.*

You Are Precious to God

You are precious and valuable, and God has a plan to manifest His goodness and kindness through what He wants to do for you. It does not matter what you have done, or what has been done to you—the past remains in the past. God has a great future for you. You can have a wonderful life, but you have to receive it. As I have said, you have to agree and say, "That is for me."

Jesus *cried out* to tell us that He has what we need: "Now on the final and most important day of the Feast, Jesus stood, and He cried in a loud voice, If any man is thirsty, let him come to Me and drink!" (John 7:37). What you cannot do for yourself, He has already done for you. He invites you now to come and receive it, to drink it, to take it into yourself. You do that by believing that it is for you.

To *drink* is defined as "to take in or receive avidly"; "to receive into one's consciousness."[14] Remember that Jesus said, "Now ask *and* keep on asking and you will receive, so that your joy (gladness, delight) may be full *and* complete" (John 16:24). If you ask and receive, *then* your joy will be full.

How are we going to impress a depressed world if we believers are as depressed as those who are without Christ? God wants His people to show forth the glory of His kindness upon them. As we receive God's provision, our joy will be complete, which is the way the Church is supposed to be.

Act as a receptacle for God's blessings. Take in what Jesus has paid for with His own life to provide for you. Study the Word so that you will be sure of His promises. Pray to Him, saying:

Here I am, Lord. Pour it on; I receive the fullness of whatever Your Holy Spirit has for me.

22

Strengthened Within

THE PURPOSE OF this book is to help you receive deliverance and freedom from the past. Whether the past is five minutes ago or fifty years ago, you will always need this message—always. You do not have to have some horrible past to need deliverance from the regrets of your past. If you get up tomorrow morning planning to be godly, and then lose your temper before breakfast, you are going to need deliverance from the past.

The devil wants to keep you trapped by some mistake you have made, or some comment you should not have said, or some sin that you have committed, or some sin that somebody has committed against you. God wants you to be delivered from what you have done and from what has been done to you—both are equally important to Him.

We have already seen from the Scriptures that Jesus came to heal the brokenhearted, to bind up our wounds, to heal our bruises. He came to give us the oil of joy instead of mourning, the garment of praise instead of heaviness, beauty instead of ashes. He came to turn us into trees of righteousness, as the planting of the Lord, so that He might be glorified (see Isaiah 61:1-3).

Jesus Himself said, "The Spirit of the Lord [is] upon Me, because He has anointed Me [the Anointed One, the Messiah] to preach the good news (the Gospel) to the poor; He has sent Me to announce release to the captives and recovery of sight to the blind, to send forth as delivered those who are oppressed [who are downtrodden, bruised, crushed, and broken down by calamity]" (Luke 4:18).

I believe that God is here with you right now; He has brought you to this time in your life to deliver you from something painful in your past. Perhaps you need deliverance from emotional wounds that were inflicted years ago, or perhaps someone recently offended you, and unforgiveness is holding you back from being all that God wants you to be. Jesus came to set all captives free. He knew that you and I would both need Him, every day.

Every time I preach this message of deliverance from a broken heart, I get stirred up to go and be all God wants me to be. I want you to be determined that you will not just be half of what God wants you to be, or three-quarters of what He wants you to be, but *all* that He wants you to be.

In Ephesians 3:16, the apostle Paul prayed, "May He grant you out of the rich treasury of His glory to be strengthened *and* reinforced with mighty power *in the inner man by the [Holy] Spirit [Himself indwelling your innermost being and personality]* (emphasis mine).

The inner man is where we need emotional healing. Our emotions are part of our soul. We are a spirit, and we have a soul. Our soul is made up of our mind, our will, and our emotions. Our mind tells us what to think, our will tells us what we want, and our emotions tell us how we feel.

Satan works to keep your emotions wounded when other people hurt you. Proverbs 18:14 KJV says, "The spirit of a man will sustain his infirmity; but a wounded spirit who can bear?" The devil wants you to remain broken inside, so that you cannot handle the trouble that comes to all of us in life.

But the Holy Spirit moves into your inner man and personality and dwells there to strengthen and reinforce you with mighty power. He reminds you of God's Word, saying, "Cast your burden on the Lord [releasing the weight of it] and He will sustain you; He will never allow the [consistently] righteous to be moved (made to slip, fall, or fail)" (Psalm 55:22).

If we have inner strength, then we can handle the problems of life. Without inner strength, we cannot even handle a traffic jam! I used to be such a mess inside that it was all I could do to deal with ordinary, everyday problems.

Our emotional wounds keep us from coping with everyday problems. We need deliverance from wounded emotions just to deal with a cranky store clerk, or a child who does not want to do what we want him to do, or a spouse who is not spiritually mature.

When we have internal problems, we have external problems. But when we are made strong inside, when we are strengthened with all might and power in the inner man, by the power of the Holy Ghost, then we can deal with all those other things that come our way.

Be Transformed into His Image

Everyone has strengths and weaknesses, and you and I are no exception. God desires to deliver us from the things that keep us in bondage to pain. He will strengthen us through the power of the Holy Spirit and will mold our personalities in such a way that we have a Spirit-controlled temperament.

If we do not receive God's help, we can become messed up in many areas of our personalities. Our natural desires oppose the nature of the Holy Spirit (see Galatians 5:17). Left to our own selfishness, we are likely to live out the practices defined in Galatians 5:19-20, which include things like strife, jealousy, and anger. Then we may get into relationships with other messed-up people and just keep distressing each other even more. But relationships are a major part of life, and we cannot avoid having to get along with other people.

The Bible is all about our relationship with God (the Godhead), our relationship with ourselves, and our relationship with others. As I said previously, if we do not like ourselves, we are never going to get along with anybody else. Many of the battles that we have with other people come because we are at war with ourselves.

The Holy Spirit is available to help mold us into the image of Christ. It is written of God in Romans 8:29: "For those whom He foreknew [of whom He was aware and loved beforehand], He also destined from the beginning [foreordaining them] to be molded into the image of His Son [and share *inwardly* His likeness], that He might become the firstborn among many brethren."

If we come to terms with the truth that we need deliverance from our wounded past, we can receive God's power to transform our personality to be like Christ, and improve our relationship with God, with ourselves, and with others. We can come to terms with our own conflicts, and receive healing in our attitude toward ourselves.

You may still blame yourself for abuses that you did not have anything to do with. The devil may be telling you there must be something wrong with you; otherwise, people would not have treated you the way they did. If you were sexually abused, the devil may be telling you that there must be something wrong with you, or else that other person or persons would not have used you for improper purposes. But you were not created for improper purposes, and any abuse you may have suffered was an injustice.

A child who is abused has no ability to look at her abuser and say, "You have a problem, and I am not your problem. You are trying to give me a problem, but I am not receiving it."

When abuse continues against us into adulthood, we find it even more difficult to defend ourselves against the devil's deceptive lies. Satan plays a recording in our thoughts that repeats:

What is wrong with me? What is wrong with me? There must be something wrong with me or this would not be happening to me. What am I doing wrong?

What am I doing wrong that you have to talk to me like that? What am I doing that you never want to put your arms around me and love me?

What am I doing that when I go to Mom or Dad for a hug, they push me away? What did I do that my parents did not even want me so that they gave me away? What am I doing that you want to treat me like your mistress instead of your daughter? What am I doing? What is wrong with me?

Nobody else I know is being treated this way. There must be something wrong with me.

Some people listen to this record of internal pain over and over, year after year after year, until suddenly they are adults looking for someone to love them because they were never offered the love they needed and deserved. They are so love-starved that they are incapable of loving anyone else the way God intended them to do.

I speak from personal experience when I say that if you still relate to that kind of internal pain, you will probably find it difficult to enter into a *normal* relationship and have *normal* expectations of anyone else. You may want your friend or spouse to make up to you for the years of abuse you suffered. But such unrealistic expectation of a friend or spouse puts them on overload and possibly scares them away. They may be trying to give you everything they know how to give you, but until you are delivered from the wounds of your past, nothing that anyone else does for you will ever be enough.

I remember going through a time when I was never happy. I always wanted Dave to do something else, always wanted him to do something more. And he sincerely tried for years. He did everything he could to help me through my crisis of pain.

Dave is a real easygoing guy, and he tried so hard to make me happy. But one day he looked at me and said, "Woman" (the only time Dave calls me "woman" is when he is fed up, which is not too often), "now hear this. I have tried to make you happy. And you know what? I have decided that it can't be done. No matter what I do, I am not going to make you happy." Then he said, "So guess what? I am finished trying."

Allow God to Fill Your Empty Heart

Thank God, the Holy Ghost was working in me through this crisis to strengthen me. I was just beginning to read the Word, and was beginning to see that all my problems, all of my present unhappiness, was not somebody else's fault—I had a problem *in* me. So I started working with God to get my life turned around.

Many married people end up in divorce when they realize that their spouse is not going to make them happy. They say, "If you're not making me happy, then I am not staying in this relationship." So they look for somebody else to make them happy, but their root of rejection keeps them brokenhearted.

A root of rejection will leave you insecure, with low self-esteem, and no confidence. Until you are delivered, you will always expect someone else to make you feel good about yourself. I needed daily fixes of self-worth, just like an addict craves his drugs. I needed reassurance all the time; there was no end to my deficiency, and sometimes, the more attention I was given, the more I craved.

People who have a root of rejection in their life feel unloved and insecure. Their personality is broken; they are shattered inside. As a result, they are constantly looking for something to make them feel okay. They try everything: a better job, a promotion, a spiritual gift, a position in the church, the right friends, the right label in their clothes, the right kind of car to drive, the right kind of house to live in, the right social group to belong to, or unending compliments. They seem to always imply, "Tell me I am okay, fall all over me with compliments, let me always be right." Insecure people cannot be corrected because they already feel so bad about themselves.

I know these things about insecure people because I had every one of these problems until *the* Counselor, the Holy Ghost, and the Word of God brought me out of that pit of despair, from ashes to beauty.

The Holy Spirit is the only One ordained to do a work within us. He fills our heart with God Himself. I encourage you to carefully consider again Paul's prayer for us, which was "[that you may really come] to know [practically, *through experience for yourselves*] the love of Christ, which far surpasses mere knowledge [without experience]; that you *may be filled [through all your being]* unto all the fullness of God [may have the richest measure of the divine Presence, *and become a body wholly filled and flooded with God Himself]!*" (Ephesians 3:19, emphasis mine).

If we become wholly filled with God Himself, we will not crave the reassurance of others. We will be so flooded with God's love that it will overflow into our relationship with Him, with ourselves, and with others.

If you will allow Him to do so, God will deliver you from

the pain of your past. Receive God's healing, and allow the Holy Spirit to have His way in your heart. He will fill you with all the reassurance that you need to enjoy life. He will show you how to put the past behind you so that you will not even feel pain if you remember it. Ecclesiastes 5:20 promises the person who totally commits himself to God: "For he shall not much remember [seriously] the days of his life, because God [Himself] answers *and* corresponds to the joy of his heart [the tranquility of God is mirrored in him]."

23

Free at Last

THE PATHWAY TO emotional healing and freedom to enjoy your life is not necessarily easy. However, pressing forward toward freedom is definitely better than staying in bondage:

> SO, SINCE Christ suffered in the flesh *for us, for you*, arm yourselves with the same thought *and* purpose [patiently to suffer rather than fail to please God]. For whoever has suffered in the flesh [having the mind of Christ] is done with [intentional] sin [has stopped pleasing himself and the world, and pleases God].
>
> So that he can no longer spend the rest of his natural life living by [his] human appetites *and* desires, but [he lives] for what God wills. (1 Peter 4:1-2)

Careful study of this Scripture passage reveals that we need to arm ourselves with proper thoughts such as: *I would prefer to suffer with Christ in order to do right, than to remain in bondage to sin.*

Having the correct mindset is important to victory. When I first realized that Jesus could and desired to set me free, I wanted to have that freedom, but my attitude was, "I will not suffer anymore; I have suffered enough, and I will not submit to anything that even remotely resembles emotional pain." The Holy Spirit led me to several scripture passages that helped me realize I had a wrong mindset and needed to prepare myself or arm myself with right thinking.

I began to think this way: *I do not want to suffer anymore, but I will do so rather than stay in bondage. As long as I am in bondage, I am suffering anyway, but it is a type of suffering that has no end. If I am willing to let Jesus lead me through whatever I must go through in order to be free, it may hurt for a while, but at least it will be a suffering that leads to victory, to a new life liberated from emotional pain.*

A good example is physical fitness. If my body were terribly out of shape due to bad eating habits and a lack of exercise, I would be suffering because I would be tired and feel bad all the time. As long as I did nothing about my condition, the suffering would just continue day after day. If I decided to get in shape, I would start to exercise, choose the right foods, and avoid the wrong ones.

For a period of time, I would suffer from sore muscles. My body might throw a fit if I did not give it certain addictive foods that it was used to. That is a type of suffering. I would need to redirect some of my time to allow for exercise, and that might produce a certain type of suffering because I would need to make wise choices and not emotional choices.

We can see by this example that in order to be free from the senseless suffering that is produced by being physically unfit, a person must suffer in another way, but it is a type of suffering that leads to victory and ultimately brings an end to suffering.

Right Suffering and Wrong Suffering

Meditating on the following scriptures reveals that we should *choose* by faith to be joyful while we are going through difficult transitions, knowing that because God loves us, even our "right suffering" will produce a good end, which is, in this case, mature character:

> Moreover [let us also be full of joy now!] let us exult *and* triumph in our troubles *and* rejoice in our sufferings, knowing that pressure *and* affliction *and* hardship produce patient *and* unswerving endurance.
>
> And endurance (fortitude) develops maturity of character (approved faith and tried integrity). And character [of this sort] produces [the habit of] joyful and confident hope of eternal salvation.
>
> Such hope never disappoints *or* deludes *or* shames us, for God's love has been poured out in our hearts through the Holy Spirit Who has been given to us. (Romans 5:3-5)

Because of a wrong mindset, many people never mature to the point that they experience joy in living. Maturity always includes stability. Without stability we never really experience peace and joy.

There is a "right suffering" and a "wrong suffering." The apostle Peter encouraged believers to be sure that they did not suffer for wrongdoing, but that if they did suffer, it should be for doing the right thing. In 1 Peter 3:14 he notes, "But . . . in case you should suffer for the sake of righteousness, [you are] blessed."

In verse 16 he exhorts us to live in such a way that we make sure that our conscience is entirely clear, and in verse 17 he says, "For [it is] better to suffer [unjustly] for doing right, if that should be God's will, than to suffer [justly] for doing wrong."

This is an important area. Many people never experience the joy of freedom because of a wrong mindset concerning suffering. At some point in your Christian life, you may have heard that Jesus wants to set you free from all your suffering, and that is true—He does. However, there is a transition involved, and transition is never easy.

During childbirth, the part of the labor process known to be the most difficult is called "transition." For thirty-three years I lived a life of pain. When I finally discovered that Jesus wanted to free me from suffering, I entered transition. I was being changed, transformed into His original idea of me before I was marred by the world. I suffered for a few more years, but in a different way. It was not a hopeless suffering but a suffering that actually produced hope, because I could see changes throughout the transition.

These were not always big changes, but the Lord always kept me from giving up. Just when I thought I could not stand the pain any longer, He would come through with a special blessing that would let me know that He was there all the time—watching over me.

The Refiner's Fire

If you understand that right suffering works like a refiner's fire, then the following verses will have special meaning that brings great comfort:

> But who can endure the day of His coming? And who can stand when He appears? For He is like a refiner's fire and like fullers' soap;

> He will sit as a refiner and purifier of silver; and He will purify the priests, the sons of Levi, and refine them like gold and silver, that they may offer to the Lord offerings in righteousness. (Malachi 3:2-3)

I would like to share with you a story that I once heard which sheds light on this passage. In Europe a man went into a goldsmith's shop and found some items he wished to buy. The entire time he was inside the shop, he never saw the shopkeeper. In order to finalize his purchases, he began to look for the proprietor, and as he did, he noticed in the rear of the shop an open door that led outside. As he stood in the doorway, he saw the shopkeeper (actually the refiner) sitting over a fire upon which sat a huge pot. He would not take his eyes off the simmering pot, even though the interested customer tried to speak to him about buying some of his merchandise.

The customer asked if he could not leave what he was doing for a short while to come inside and take care of the transaction. However, the refiner said, "No." He stated that he could not leave the metal in the pot, not even for one minute, explaining it this way: "It is very important that this metal, which is gold, does not harden until all the impurities are out of it. I intend for it to be pure gold. If the fire gets too hot, it could ruin it, and if the fire gets too cool, the gold could harden with impurities still in it."

He explained that he could not leave it, nor take his eyes off it at all. He would need to sit over it until it was completely finished. The customer asked when that would be, and the refiner replied, "I will know it is finished when I can look in the metal and see my reflection very clearly."

To me, this is such a beautiful story because it lets me know that God is always guarding my life and watching over the trials that come my way to make sure they do not become too intense. But He also makes sure there is enough pressure to keep doing a work in me.

In 1 Corinthians 10:13 Paul says that God will never allow more to come upon us than we can bear, but with every temptation He will also provide a way out. We can trust God not to expect us to endure beyond our ability.

Believe me, God knows what you are capable of bearing even more than you do. Trust Him, and He will bring you through the refining process so that you emerge as pure gold.

PRESS ON TOWARD THE GOAL

It will be easier to endure right suffering if you understand that the refiner's fire is a lifelong process. Realizing this truth, the apostle Paul wrote: "Not that I have now attained [this ideal], or have already been made perfect, but I press on to lay hold of (grasp) *and* make my own, that for which Christ Jesus . . . has laid hold of me" (Philippians 3:12).

In his writings, Paul often likens the Christian life to a race:

> Do you not know that in a race all the runners compete, but [only] one receives the prize? So run [your race] that you may lay hold [of the prize] *and* make it yours.
>
> Now every athlete who goes into training conducts himself temperately *and* restricts himself in all things. They do it to win a wreath that will soon wither, but we [do it to receive a crown of eternal blessedness] that cannot wither.
>
> Therefore I do not run uncertainly (without definite aim). I do not box like one beating the air *and* striking without an adversary.
>
> But [like a boxer] I buffet my body [handle it roughly, discipline it by hardships] and subdue it, for fear that after

> proclaiming to others the Gospel *and* things pertaining to it, I myself should become unfit [not stand the test, be unapproved and rejected as a counterfeit]. (1 Corinthians 9:24-27)

Trust the Lord, and He will bring you across the finish line. Be determined to press on and to take hold of that for which Christ has taken hold of you. He took hold of you to save you.

Your salvation included many benefits in this life—not just a home in heaven when you die. Your eternal salvation began the day you were born again, and it will never end. God took hold of you to restore to you what the enemy had stolen from you, but you will need to be determined to have it back.

Do not be passive and expect victory to just fall on you. It does come by the grace of God, and not by our works, but we must actively cooperate with the Holy Spirit each step of the way.

In his book, *The Great Lover's Manifesto*, Dave Grant points out that we never grow when things are easy. We waste away without effort. We human beings are essentially lazy and always searching for the easy way, but in reality, we need some tension in order to stretch and grow. We will not grow until we agree that struggle benefits us, and that struggle is good because it keeps us moving and alive. Paul said that he "pressed on." His phrase indicated tension and struggle; it indicated that the Christian walk is not easy.

In Grant's book, he relates the following story: "A number of bees were taken along on a flight into space in order to see how they would handle the experience of weightlessness. In the weightless atmosphere they were able to float in space without any effort. The report on the experiment was summed up in these words: '*They enjoyed the ride, but they died*'" (emphasis mine).[15] I agree 100 percent with Mr. Grant, who goes on to say that we seldom *drift* into anything worthwhile.

Hang Tough in Hard Times!

In the following verses, the Old Testament prophet Habakkuk speaks of hard times, which he calls "high places," and states that God had given him hinds' feet to remain surefooted during those times:

> Though the fig tree does not blossom and there is no fruit on the vines, [though] the product of the olive fails and the fields yield no food, though the flock is cut off from the fold and there are no cattle in the stalls,
>
> Yet I will rejoice in the Lord; I will exult in the [victorious] God of my salvation!
>
> The Lord God is my Strength, my personal bravery, *and* my invincible army; He makes my feet like hinds' feet and will make me to walk [not to stand still in terror, but to walk] *and* make [spiritual] progress upon my high places [of trouble, suffering, or responsibility]! (Habakkuk 3:17-19)

The term *hind* refers to a certain kind of deer that is an agile mountain climber. It can scale up what looks like a sheer cliff with no difficulty at all, leaping from ledge to ledge with great ease. This surefootedness is God's will for us, so that when hardship comes our way we are not intimidated nor frightened at all.

To be truly victorious, we must grow to the place where we are not afraid of hard times but are actually challenged by them. In these verses, *The Amplified Bible* refers to these "high places" as "trouble, suffering, or responsibility." This is because it is during these times that we grow.

If you look back over your life, you will see that you never grow during easy times; you grow during hard times. During the easy times that come, you are able to enjoy what you have gained during the hard times. This is really a life principle; it is just the way it works. You work all week, then you receive your paycheck and enjoy your weekend off. You exercise, eat right, and take good care of yourself, then you enjoy a healthy body. You clean your house, or basement, or garage, and then you enjoy your neat, clean surroundings each time you walk through them.

I am reminded of Hebrews 12:11: "For the time being no discipline brings joy, but seems grievous *and* painful; but afterwards it yields a peaceable fruit of righteousness to those who have been trained by it."

The person who serves God from love for Him does what is right because it is right. He does not do it to inherit any good, though in the end the blessing will not fail him. Seek to be whole in order to give the Lord glory, and in the end, you will enjoy being glorious.

24

Build Bridges—Not Walls

WALLS REPRESENT PROTECTION. We all have a tendency to build our own walls in an attempt to protect ourselves against being hurt. As I have mentioned several times, although I have a very kind and wonderful husband, there are times when he hurts me. I finally realized that whenever my husband caused me emotional pain, I erected a wall—I am speaking spiritually—behind which I could hide and keep him from hurting me again. But the Holy Spirit showed me that when I put up walls to keep others out, I also wall myself into a solitary place of confinement.

Many people live isolated lives because they have erected self-made walls to protect themselves. However, those walls become prisons, and they are trapped in bitterness and loneliness. They erect protective walls to prevent themselves from experiencing emotional pain, but they are unable to love and be loved unless they are willing to be hurt.

Spending your lifetime trying to avoid pain is more painful than living normally and dealing with each issue as it arises.

Jesus is the Healer and will always be available to minister comfort to you in hurtful situations.

I believe the Lord wants me to encourage you right now to take a step of faith and tear down your self-made walls. The thought will probably be frightening, especially if you have been living behind them for a long time. God can bring down those emotional walls that separate you from others, just as He crumbled the walls of Jericho (see Joshua 2:1-21; 6:1-27). The *King James Version* of Hebrews 11:30 states that "by faith" the walls came down.

I have to take a step of faith each time Jesus shows me that I have erected walls to keep others out. I must choose to put my faith in Him as my Protector, rather than attempting to protect myself.

There are several scriptures in the Bible that promise God's protection. Isaiah 60:18 is one that ministers to me: "Violence shall no more be heard in your land, nor devastation or destruction within your borders, but you shall call your walls Salvation and your gates Praise."

What this verse says to me is that salvation through Jesus Christ is a wall of protection about me. From the moment I become His, He takes upon Himself the job of protecting me. However, in order to activate the blessings in my life, I must believe that He is watching over me. As long as I continue to reject the Lord's protection, trying to take care of myself, I will continue to live in bondage and misery.

Another wonderful scripture on the subject of God's protection is Isaiah 30:18: "And therefore the Lord [earnestly] waits [expecting, looking, and longing] to be gracious to you; and therefore He lifts Himself up, that He may have mercy on you *and* show loving-kindness to you. For the Lord is a God of justice. Blessed (happy, fortunate, to be envied) are all those who [earnestly] wait for Him, who expect *and* look *and* long for Him [for His victory, His favor, His love, His peace, His joy, and His matchless, unbroken companionship]!"

Careful study of this verse reveals God as One Who is literally waiting for an opportunity to be good to us, to bring justice into our situations. However, He can do that only for those who are expecting and waiting for Him to do so. Give up the labor of "self-protection" and start allowing and expecting God to protect you.

Let God be God.

As you enter this new realm, by faith, I cannot promise that you will never be hurt, but I can promise that God is "a God of justice," which means that He will eventually bring balance and will reward you for choosing His way.

Any person who chooses God's way to handle his problems and hurtful situations is destined for great things: "Even as it is written . . . we are regarded *and* counted as sheep for the slaughter. Yet amid all these *things we are more than conquerors and* gain a surpassing victory through Him Who loved us" (Romans 8:36, 37, emphasis mine).

How can we be more than conquerors, and at the same time look like sheep being led to the slaughter? The answer is simple: While it may appear we are being taken advantage of, while it may seem that the Lord is not going to rescue us, we are more than conquerors because in "the midst of the mess," we have a knowing inside that our God will never leave us nor forsake us and that, at exactly the right moment, our deliverance and reward will come.

Building Bridges

One day while I was praying, the Holy Spirit showed me that my life had become a bridge for others to pass over and find their place in God. For many years, I erected only walls in my life, but now where there were walls there are bridges instead. All the difficult and unfair things that have happened to me have been turned into highways over which others can pass to find the same liberty that I have found.

I have learned to build bridges instead of walls.

As I stated in the fifth chapter of this book, God is no respecter of persons (see Acts 10:34). What He does for one, He will do for another, as long as His precepts are followed. If you will follow the precepts that have been outlined in these pages, you will discover the same freedom that I have found. Then you can become a bridge for others to pass over, instead of a wall that shuts them out.

In Hebrews 5:9 Jesus is referred to as "the Author *and* Source of eternal salvation." He pioneered a pathway to God for us. He became a highway for us to pass over. It is as though He faced a giant forest and went in ahead of us so that when we came along we could drive right through it without having to fight all the elements and the density of the forest. He sacrificed Himself for us, and now that we are benefiting from His sacrifice, He is giving us a chance to sacrifice for others so they can reap the same benefits we enjoy.

Hebrews 12:2 says that Jesus endured the cross for the joy of obtaining the prize that was set before Him. I like to remind myself of that fact when the way seems hard. I tell myself, "Keep pressing on, Joyce; there is joy ahead."

Make a decision to tear down your walls and build bridges. There are many, many people who are lost in their messes and need someone to go before them and show them the way. Why not be that person for them?

Walls or bridges? The choice is yours.

Beauty for Ashes

Not only does the Lord want to turn your walls into bridges, but as He promises in His Word, He also wants to give you beauty for ashes:

> THE SPIRIT of the Lord God is upon me, because the Lord has anointed *and* qualified me to preach the Gospel *of* good tidings to the meek, the poor, *and* afflicted; He has sent me to bind up *and* heal the brokenhearted, to proclaim liberty to the [physical and spiritual] captives and the opening of the prison *and* of the eyes to those who are bound, to proclaim the acceptable year of the Lord [the year of His favor] . . . To grant [consolation and joy] to those who mourn (in Zion) . . . to give them an ornament (a garland or diadem) of beauty instead of ashes, the oil of joy instead of mourning, the garment [expressive] of praise instead of a heavy, burdened, *and* failing spirit. (Isaiah 61:1, 2, 3)

These promises in Isaiah 61 are rich and plentiful. Read them and make a decision not to miss out on a single one. I will be in agreement with you as I pray that every person who reads this book will inherit the promises.

God has done His part by giving us Jesus. I have done my part by acting on the Word of God and obtaining freedom, then writing this book to help you do the same. Now, you must do your part by making a quality decision that you will never give up until you have allowed Him to:

> bind up your wounds;
> heal your broken heart;
> liberate you in every area of your life;
> open your prison door;

give you joy instead of mourning,
a garment of praise instead of a heavy,
burdened and failing spirit;
    and
beauty instead of ashes.

25

Nothing Will Be Wasted

No experience in your life is ever wasted or in vain if you give all your cares to the Lord. Even if your fragmented life looks like an abandoned battlefield, Jesus can reshape all the pieces of your past into something beautiful.

After Jesus had fed five thousand people with just a few loaves of bread and two small fish, He told His disciples, "Gather up now the fragments (the broken pieces that are left over), so that nothing may be lost *and* wasted" (John 6:12). The disciples gathered up twelve baskets of food from the left-overs, still much more than the small offering of loaves and fishes that was made to Jesus in the first place.

God set me free from fear, insecurity, emotional addictions, and the bondage of a deep-rooted sense of rejection. Then He reshaped my fragmented life and gave me the glorious privilege of teaching His people how they can be whole; how they can have fruitful, happy lives and ministries; and how they can enjoy healthy, loving relationships.

I have learned to receive unconditional love from God, from Dave, and even from myself. My husband does not do everything I want him to, the way I want him to, when I want him to; but that is okay now, because I have learned how to love him unconditionally too.

When we were first married, I did not know anything about unconditional love. My family had to do everything my way, or else I assumed they did not love me.

When I suffered from a broken heart, everyone who was in a relationship with me had to work very hard to try to keep me happy. They suffered because they could never be real with me. They could never honestly tell me the truth about anything. They had to tell me what I wanted to hear if they wanted any peace at all.

If I said to Dave, "Let's go get a cup of coffee," he could not say, "Well, I would rather not do that," or I would pout. That was my way of controlling things. I was broken: shattered, fractured, fragmented, and dysfunctional. I had been violated, and I was making everyone pay for my pain, even if they were not the ones who had caused it.

If you have been violated through abuse, your rights as a human being were dishonored, which can cause you to feel overwhelmed. So many victims of abuse eventually reach the point where they say, "I can't handle this." They are not really troubled by the problems in everyday life; they are overwhelmed by the problems of a broken heart. Those of us who grew up in a dysfunctional home are often so insecure that we create dysfunctional homes too.

We need inner strength to keep from being overwhelmed by outward circumstances. We must allow God to gather up our fragmented dreams and remold us into the image of Christ. To do that, He may have to crush the few pieces we have left into fine clay, water us with His Word, reshape our lumpy mass of leftovers, and put us back on His potter's wheel. But He is more than capable of designing something miraculous from whatever we have left to give Him.

Jesus told us that in the world there would be trouble, saying, "I have told you these things, so that in Me you may have [perfect] peace *and* confidence. In the world you have tribulation *and* trials *and* distress *and* frustration; but be of good cheer [take courage; be confident, certain, undaunted]! For I have overcome the world. [I have deprived it of power to harm you and have conquered it for you]" (John 16:33).

Nobody can avoid tribulation in this life, but those who put their faith in Jesus can be of good cheer: "Many *are* the afflictions of the righteous: but the LORD delivereth him out of them all" (Psalm 34:19 KJV). But the Word does not say that God delivers us immediately. We may have to go through a few things first.

Life always overcomes death, and light always overcomes darkness. Without God's Word, the future may seem dark, but Jesus said that He came to deliver us from darkness: "I have come as a Light into the world, so that whoever believes in Me [whoever cleaves to *and* trusts in *and* relies on Me] may not continue to live in darkness" (John 12:46). Instead of living in darkness and misery, we are to *continue* to follow Jesus and conform wholly to His example in living (see John 12:26).

You cannot *continue* if you are broken, overwhelmed, or subdued. But by now, you have received enough of God's Word through the testimonies in this book, to know that you are no longer bound to your past, if you follow the Lord. Jesus said, "If you abide in My word [hold fast to My teachings and live in accordance with them], you are truly My disciples. And you will know the Truth, and the Truth will set you free" (John 8:31-32).

Continue to Follow the Lord

God plants dreams in people's hearts. But many people do not continue all the way to the end in order to follow Him to the fulfillment of that dream. Many get started and quit, get started and quit, get started and quit. They do not continue because their broken heart overwhelms their hope. They do not have any inner strength to carry them through to the end.

Jesus will bind up your wounds and heal your bruises. His Word is medicine for your soul (see Proverbs 4:20-22). Read the Word of God every day, even if you read only one verse each day. I encourage you to read my daily devotional, *Starting Your Day Right*, and then as you fall asleep at night, think God-inspired thoughts, such as: *I am the righteousness of God in Jesus Christ. God loves me. He has a good plan for my future.* Then pray faith-filled prayers such as this:

Lord, I believe that You love me and that You can take up all these broken pieces of my life and make something out of them for my good. In Romans 8:28 Your Word says, "All things work together and are [fitting into a plan] for good to and for those who love God and are called according to [His] design and purpose." I love You, Lord. I believe that You forgive me. Father, I receive Your healing for my broken heart.

Do not go to bed at night thinking what a horrible mess you are in and how you will never overcome it, or how nothing will ever get any better, or how nothing will ever be any different. Take the Word as your medicine. It is medicine for your flesh, your soul, and your spirit. Study it so that the power of the Word and the Spirit can work together in your life.

When you read a verse in the Bible that you want to appropriate for yourself, add it to your prayers. For example, Psalm 30:11-12 can become part of your bedtime praises; along with the psalmist you can worship God by praying: *You have turned my mourning into dancing for me; You have put off my sackcloth and girded me with gladness, to the end that my tongue and my heart and everything glorious within me may sing praise to You and not be silent. O Lord my God, I will give thanks to You forever.*

God is eager to pour out His Spirit into your life. Just pray, *Lord, move in my life. Do whatever You want to do. Heal the people I have hurt, and heal me too.*

YOUR PAIN WILL NOT BE WASTED

As a child I was never able to be carefree, never able to live without worries, never able just to wake up and play. I always felt sorry for myself because it seemed that my childhood and teenage years were just wasted. And then I was in a bad marriage for five years, and I felt that was a waste. As an adult, I felt that I had spent so many years just wasting my life. But God gathered up those wasted years and made my mess become my message.

He found value in every sad situation I lived through. You may be wondering, *How could God ever make anything good out of this mess that I have created?* God has ways that we know nothing about. He is using all of my wasted years to reach the thousands upon thousands of people who say to me, "I listen to you every day."

Sometimes I marvel at what they are listening to. They hear me tell about what a mess I used to be and how God made me whole again, and that message is giving them hope and faith that He will do the same for them. He is getting value out of my brokenness by using it to heal other peoples' brokenness.

Maybe you feel that you have wasted your life until now, but spending your time thinking about it does not move you to a new place. If you trust God, He can do something glorious in whatever time you have left, even if it is only a short while. God can do something so glorious in the time that you have remaining that everything you went through will have been worth it just to see God take it and do what He can do in you.

It is impossible for me to be doing what I am doing today. When God called me into ministry, to say I was a mess does not even accurately describe it. But I loved God, and I did not want to continue being the way I was. I just did not know how to change the way I was and be different and better. It took years for God to get me where He needed me to be, but I believe that He is doing a quicker work of righteousness in these last days.

God Will Do What Seems Impossible

Even if it takes decades, it is better to be on your way up than on your way down. Pray, *Okay God, here. Take my broken life and gather up the fragments so that nothing in it will be wasted.* Do not remain broken; make a decision to trust your past and your future to the Lord.

You may feel the way Martha felt when her brother Lazarus died. She said to Jesus, "Master, if You had been here, my brother would not have died" (John 11:21). Jesus could have arrived on the scene sooner, but the Bible says that He purposely waited until Lazarus was dead and laid in the grave. He waited until the situation was so impossible that if anything good came of it, everybody would know that it had to be a work of God (see John 11:1-11).

We need to understand that when God does not move in our circumstances, or when He does not move as quickly as we would like for Him to move, He may be waiting on purpose. Just when we think there is no way out of our mess, God will prove to us how strong and wonderful He is on our behalf (See 2 Chronicles 16:9).

I had been trying to serve God for years. Why did He wait so long to touch me with the power of the Holy Ghost? Why didn't He do it two years before? Four years before? I think He was just waiting until it would take a miracle to prove that He was working in my life. The fact that God could use my life for ministry is a miracle in itself.

If Jesus had put His twelve chosen disciples through personality tests, the results would have indicated that they did not have the qualities needed to make a good ministry team. The analysts would have advised Jesus to continue His search for men who were more suited for the work He was going to require of them. Their reports would have read, "Peter is emotionally unstable and given to fits of temper, and Thomas is full of doubt," and one by one, each disciple would have been similarly disqualified.

It is interesting to note that before Jesus chose these twelve men (see Luke 6:12-16), He prayed all night! I wonder how long He prayed before He chose you and me to do what we are called to do. Jesus knows all about each one of us, yet He picked us anyway. Why? He wants to heal the brokenhearted. He wants to gather up the fragments and show His power. And the weaker the people He chooses, the greater His power is visible through them.

When I first started serving God, I spent half of every week crying in self-pity. In spite of that fact, I was still anointed to teach Bible studies; I could preach then just as well as I can right now. But God kept me trapped in my living room with twenty-five people for years before He began to lead me into the worldwide ministry I have today.

I learned that God would not release me for public ministry until I had let Him do a work in my most private life. But during all that time of faithfulness to little things, I was progressing little by little, from glory to glory (2 Corinthians 3:18 KJV).

The great thing about God is that He does not just see where we are, He also sees where we are going. And He treats us with the end in mind throughout the whole trip. He loves us with an unconditional love from the beginning of our relationship. We may try to get His love every way imaginable, but all we need to do is *receive* it.

Sometimes we try so hard to get into the presence of God, but the truth is that it is impossible to get away from Him. He is in constant pursuit of us.

In Psalm 139:7-10 the psalmist wrote of God:

> Where could I go from Your Spirit? Or where could I flee from Your presence?
>
> If I ascend up into heaven, You are there; if I make my bed in Sheol (the place of the dead), behold, You are there.
>
> If I take the wings of the morning or dwell in the uttermost parts of the sea,
>
> Even there shall Your hand lead me, and Your right hand shall hold me.

In verse 16 of this passage, the psalmist says that all the days of our lives "were written before ever they took shape, when as yet there was none of them." And in verses 17 and 18, he says that God thinks about us all the time: "How precious *and* weighty also are Your thoughts to me, O God! How vast is the sum of them! If I could count them, they would be more in number than the sand."

Do not determine your self-worth by how others have treated you. Receive your worth and value from who you are in Christ.

You may sometimes feel that the Lord is not near, but that is why knowing the Word is so important. The prophet Isaiah brought a complaint before the Lord, reporting that His people were saying:

"The Lord has forsaken me, and my Lord has forgotten me."

> [And the Lord answered] "Can a woman forget her nursing child, that she should not have compassion on the son of her womb? Yes, they may forget, yet I will not forget you.
>
> Behold, I have indelibly imprinted (tattooed a picture of) you on the palm of each of My hands" (Isaiah 49:14-16).

Parents did not originate the idea of keeping pictures of their children handy—God carries a picture of His children everywhere He goes. The next time you question your self-worth, remember that God has your picture tattooed on the palms of His hands.

26

Double for Your Trouble

NO MATTER WHAT you have gone through, if you stick close to God, He will reward you. The Word says in Hebrews 11:6, "But without faith it is impossible to please *and* be satisfactory to Him. For whoever would come near to God must [necessarily] believe that God exists and that He is the rewarder of those who earnestly *and* diligently seek Him [out]."

Many people seem to believe that God is a punisher. But they obviously do not have an intimate knowledge of God. By His very nature of love (see 1 John 4:8), God is a rewarder.

God wants us to *expect* a reward; He wants us to believe for and look forward to His reward. His Word says that those who come to Him must believe that He is and that He is a rewarder. We should not focus on what we have been through; we should set our thoughts on what God is going to do for us, as we remain faithful to Him. Our testimony should be filled with praise for Him as we proclaim, "I have a reward coming!"

The expectation of a reward fills us with hope. It helps us get through difficulties. The Bible says that although Jesus despised the cross, He endured it for the joy of the prize that was on the other side of it. Consequently, we are to continue "looking away [from all that will distract] to Jesus, Who is the Leader *and* the Source of our faith [giving the first incentive for our belief] and is also its Finisher [bringing it to maturity and perfection]" (Hebrews 12:2).

Nobody would want to go to work if they did not think they were going to get a paycheck. When there is a prize for endurance, there is motivation in us that gives us the stamina to keep going. We say, "It's okay; I can go through this, because I know I'm going to get something out of it."

It is important to realize that God is a loving Father and that He is going to take care of us. We are faithful to Him because of His goodness to us. He brings a reward and special blessings into our lives, not because He owes us anything but because it is His very nature to demonstrate love to those who diligently seek Him.

If you were not diligently seeking after more of God, you would have put this message aside many pages ago. But here you are, still reading, hoping to learn something about God that you did not know before. That tells me that you are in line for a reward from Him, as one who is faithfully seeking the Lord.

God Is Watching You

God is watching you, and He sees everything you do. The psalmist said of Him, "You know my downsitting and my uprising; You understand my thought afar off" (Psalm 139:2). The Bible says, "For the eyes of the Lord run to and fro throughout the whole earth to show Himself strong in behalf of those whose hearts are blameless toward Him" (2 Chronicles 16:9). God is eagerly seeking opportunities to reward you for your faith in Him.

Jesus said, "Behold, I am coming soon, and I shall bring My wages *and* rewards with Me, to repay *and* render to each one just what his own actions *and* his own work merit" (Revelation 22:12). That means that people will receive pay for the actions they commit while on this earth. Now, that can be exciting in one way, and frightening in another way. We need to realize that God is watching us, and that no one is really getting by with anything.

God neither sleeps nor slumbers (see Psalm 121:4). He knows everything that goes on behind closed doors. So we need to live as if we really believe that God is watching our every move. When we sit and have a conversation, we need to remember that God is the unseen Guest Who is listening to everything that we have to say.

Jesus warned His followers:

> TAKE CARE not to do your good deeds publicly *or* before men, in order to be seen by them; otherwise you will have no reward [reserved for and awaiting you] with *and* from your Father Who is in heaven. Thus, whenever you give to the poor, do not blow a trumpet before you, as the hypocrites in the synagogues and in the streets like to do, that they may be recognized *and* honored *and* praised by men. Truly I tell you, they have their reward in full already. (Matthew 6:1-2)

If we do things to get attention from people, then the public attention we receive from others is our reward, and there will be no further reward from God. Do not trade God's reward for people's reward. Wait for what God can give you, because it is going to be much better than the reward that people can give you.

Jesus went on to say, "But when you give to charity, do not let your left hand know what your right hand is doing, so that your deeds of charity may be in secret; and your Father Who sees in secret will reward you *openly*" (Matthew 6:3-4).

In other words, do good works with pure motives, but do not boast about them. What you are able to do secretly, God will reward you for openly. Jesus even told us to pray privately, saying, "But when you pray, go into your [most] private room, and, closing the door, pray to your Father, Who is in secret; and your Father, Who sees in secret, will reward you *in the open*" (Matthew 6:6).

You may feel that you have a thankless job. Maybe you have worked in the church nursery for ten years, and the only feedback you ever get is from a few parents who complain about the way you take care of their kids. Or maybe you have been ushering at the church for five years, and nobody has ever said thank you for your faithfulness. Or maybe you are an intercessor, and nobody even knows that you are praying for them. But you are motivated to do what you do "as unto the Lord."

Do not become discouraged in doing good, for God sees everything you are doing for others on His behalf. Not one good work that you do with the right motive has gone unnoticed by Him. God sees every person you help, every person you are kind to; He knows every time you show somebody a little bit of mercy, every time you show someone forgiveness; and He will reward you for it. If you are looking forward to God's reward, you will continue to do things with the right motive.

What to Do When Trouble Comes

Sooner or later we all have some trouble in life. We all have some trials and some tribulations. Everybody goes through times of testing. And not every storm shows up in the forecast.

Some days we can wake up and think everything is going to be great. Before that day is over, we may be tested by all kinds of trouble that we were not expecting.

Trouble is part of life, so we simply have to be ready for it. We need to have a planned response to trouble, because it is more difficult to get strong after trouble comes. It is better to be prepared by staying strong.

The first thing you need to do when trouble comes is pray, *God, help me stay emotionally stable.* Do not let your emotions overwhelm you. The next thing you need to do is trust God. The instant that fear rises up, pray.

Stay emotionally stable, trust God, and pray. Then while you are waiting for God to answer, simply keep doing good. Keep your commitments. Do not stop serving the Lord just because you have a problem. The greatest time in the world to keep your commitments to God is in the midst of difficulty and adversity. When the devil sees that trials and tribulations won't stop you, he will stop troubling you for a while.

"And let us not lose heart *and* grow weary *and* faint in acting nobly *and* doing right, for in due time *and* at the appointed season we shall reap, if we do not loosen *and* relax our courage *and* faint" (Galatians 6:9).

So there are four things to do when trouble and trials come to you: Stay emotionally stable; trust God; pray immediately to avoid getting into fear; and keep doing good. The fifth thing to do is *expect a reward.*

We seldom even do one of these things when trouble comes, but that may be from not having a plan. I believe we need to stay strong by practicing these steps even when we are not in trouble.

To be prepared for the next time you find yourself in a difficult situation, practice saying, "I am going to be faithful to God, and God is going to give me double for my trouble. Satan, you thought you were going to hurt me, but I am going to get a double blessing, because I am one who diligently seeks the Lord."

God's Will for You

This is the will of God concerning you: Double blessings are in store for you, because you believe that "He is the rewarder of those who earnestly *and* diligently seek Him [out]" (Hebrews 11:6).

As you can see, there is a condition—and that is to believe. Where there is a privilege, there is also a responsibility. If you do your part, God will never fail to do His part.

You will have trouble, but what matters is how you respond to it. Do not get discouraged, disappointed, depressed, negative, or hopeless when trials come. Instead, just shake them off and keep on going. There is an upside to trouble. When you have trouble, you experience the comfort of God.

Jesus said, "Blessed *and* enviably happy [with a happiness produced by the experience of God's favor and especially conditioned by the revelation of His matchless grace] are those who mourn, for they shall be comforted!" (Matthew 5:4).

If we really understand how awesome the comfort of God is, it is almost worth it to have a problem just to experience His marvelous comfort. The Bible says, "Blessed be the God and Father of our Lord Jesus Christ, the Father of sympathy (pity and mercy) and the God [Who is the Source] of every comfort (consolation and encouragement), Who comforts (consoles and encourages) us in every trouble (calamity and affliction), so that we may also be able to comfort (console and encourage) those who are in any kind of trouble *or* distress, with the comfort (consolation and encouragement) with which we ourselves are comforted (consoled and encouraged) by God" (2 Corinthians 1:3-4).

God comforts us so we can comfort others.

Enjoy God's Favor

Something else we need to confess every day of our life is, "I have favor with God, and God gives me favor with man. I walk in the favor of God." When you have God's favor, people like you and want to do things for you, and they don't even know why. There is no natural reason, but they are drawn to you and want to be good to you; they just want to be a blessing to you.

God's favor is wonderful. People who have been abused need to learn to shake off their offenses and just enjoy this free gift of grace from God. Those who humble themselves enjoy more and more favor in their lives.

Peter was someone who was easily offended but who learned to humble himself and enjoy God's favor in His life.

God's Blessings Are Bigger Than You Can Imagine

If I had not learned to cast my cares on the Lord, and let Him strengthen and settle me, I would not be enjoying the double blessings through which we now minister. When God called us to go on television, the Spirit of God visited Dave one morning as he was combing his hair. He said to Dave, "I have prepared you and Joyce all this time to go on television."

We didn't know that we were in a time of preparation during all those years when we were faithful to travel anywhere to hold meetings for fifty to a hundred people; to sleep in Mc-

Donald's parking lots when we didn't have the money to stay in hotels, because we were willing to preach for little to nothing; to withstand judgment and criticism, and endure rejection from our home church. It was all preparation for a greater work.

We knew to stay faithful, but we never dreamed God's reward would be this big. We now enjoy preaching the Word to audiences of several thousand people at a time who are hungry to know God more intimately. Our *Life In The Word* telecast is aired daily over 400 television stations, with a potential audience of 2.5 billion people in nearly two-thirds of the world. Since 1988, we have released more than fifty books, thirty-six of which have been translated into forty-five languages, and have distributed over 3 million copies. I boast only of the Lord; God had a reward in mind for us, and His blessings upon us continue to expand each year.

I didn't know this is what God had in mind when He was telling me, "Just hang on, Joyce, I am going to give you double for your trouble. What the devil meant for evil against you, I am turning for good so that you will be in a position to help many people."

God has the same message for everybody. We must endure times of preparation, but we can be "assured *and* know that [God being a partner in their labor] all things work together *and* are [fitting into a plan] for good to *and* for those who love God and are called according to [His] design *and* purpose" (Romans 8:28).

So the next time you face trouble, shake it off. If you are loving God and walking in His will for your life to the best of your ability, then you can be assured that everything is going to work out for your good. We serve a good God Who takes bad things and works them out for good.

God's Great Exchange

God is in the exchange business; He takes all the junk that we do not want and exchanges it for all the good that He has in store for us.

For example, when I married Dave, I did not have any money. I did not have a car but Dave had a car. When we got married, suddenly I had a car and money, because when Dave and I were married, everything he had suddenly became mine too.

It is the same way when we commit to Jesus. He is the Bridegroom, and we are His bride. We do not become heirs to His promise by simply *dating* Him, but by fully committing ourselves to Him as in a marriage. A lot of people want to just "date" Jesus, hoping they will still get the double blessings.

The power that is in the name of Jesus is enjoyed only by those who *belong* to Him. I did not get Dave's name until I married him. When you come to the Lord and commit everything in your life to Him, complete with its pain and injustices, God promises to take everything that is wrong in it and exchange it for what is right.

Jesus said:

> If you [really] love Me, you will keep (obey) My commands" (John 14:15). Those who love Him and obey Him will receive His great exchange described in Isaiah 61:7: "Instead of your [former] shame you shall have a twofold recompense; instead of dishonor *and* reproach [your people] shall rejoice in their portion. Therefore in their land they shall possess double [what they had forfeited]; everlasting joy shall be theirs."

27

Shake It Off

THERE WILL ALWAYS be new opportunities to apply the principles of letting go of the past and pressing on for God's prize that we have discussed in this book. Someone who matters to you will inevitably do something to hurt you. When that happens, you will have to choose again to receive God's love, forgive the one who hurt you, pray for him, bless him, believe that God will turn the situation around for your good, and then wait for the prize of His reward.

To encourage your faith to press on to the higher prize of freedom from emotional pain, God has included many stories of victory in the Bible to remind you of people who learned to shake off offenses and remain faithful to the Lord. In fact, the Bible is full of stories of those who received double blessings for being faithful.

Joseph went from the pit to the palace. Daniel went from the lions' den to a place of promotion.

Ruth started out eating scraps in a field, because she was faithful to a mother-in-law who was going to be alone without her. Their husbands were dead, and Ruth could have gone back to the security of her own people. Her mother-in-law told her, "Just go back." But she said, "No, I'm staying with you, and your people shall be my people, and your God shall be my God" (see Ruth 1:16). Then God gave her favor, and Ruth ended up marrying Boaz, who just happened to be the richest man in the country.

Esther started out as a frightened young maiden, who was not really happy about the position she was offered. But she was obedient to what God was leading her to do, and she went from being an orphan to a queen who saved a whole nation of people.

And then, of course, there is the story of Job.

The amazing thing about Job is that God allowed him to go through the painful experiences he suffered because God knew he would make it through them successfully. He knew Job was a man He could trust. If you have never read the entire book of Job, I encourage you to do so.

The devil thought that Job was faithful to God only because God protected him. So God said to Satan, "Okay then, we will remove some of that protection, and you will find that he will still stay faithful to me" (see Job 1:12). So God allowed Satan to attack and destroy every good thing that Job possessed. He took *everything* away from him except his life, but Job still would not deny his allegiance to the Lord.

As a result of Job's faithfulness, "the Lord turned the captivity of Job *and* restored his fortunes, when he prayed for his friends; also the Lord gave Job twice as much as he had before" (Job 42:10). It is important to note that the Lord turned Job's captivity and restored his fortunes *when* he prayed for his friends. These were the same "friends" who had severely disappointed him, who had not been there for him, and who had judged and criticized him. But the Lord gave Job twice as much as he had before, because he was faithful to continue doing the right thing even though it was painful.

The Lord gave Job twice as much as he had before all the trouble started. God gave him a double blessing for all the trouble he had been through. Verses 12 and 13 of Job 42 say: "And the Lord blessed the latter days of Job more than his beginning; for he had 14,000 sheep, 6,000 camels, 1,000 yoke of oxen, and 1,000 female donkeys. He had also seven sons and three daughters."

Now, you may not want sheep or camels, oxen or donkeys, or even more kids, but God knows what kind of double blessing to give to you for your faithfulness. But in order to keep pressing on and reap your double blessing, you will have to learn to shake off the troubles that come your way.

One of my favorite stories is about a farmer's donkey that fell into a dry well. The animal cried pitifully for hours as the farmer tried to figure out what to do for his poor donkey. Finally, he concluded that the well was too deep, and it really needed to be covered up anyway; besides, the donkey was old, and it would be a lot of trouble to get him out of the pit. The farmer decided that it was not worth trying to retrieve the animal, so he asked his neighbors to help him fill in the well and bury the donkey.

They all grabbed shovels and began to toss dirt into the well. The donkey immediately realized what was happening, and he began to weep horribly. Crying would be our normal response if somebody was mistreating us this badly, so this donkey was responding the same way we would at first, but then he got real quiet. A few shovel loads of dirt later, the farmer looked down the well and was astonished at what he saw. With every shovel of dirt that hit the donkey's back, the donkey would shake it off, and step on top of it.

As the neighbors and the farmer continued to shovel dirt on top of the animal, he would continue to shake it off, and take a step up. Pretty soon the donkey shook off the last shovel full of dirt, took a step up, and walked right out of the well.

We can learn so much from this story. When trouble comes, if we will quit moaning long enough to get still and listen, God will tell us what to do about our trouble.

By the grace and the mercy of God, I was able to shake off a lot of things in my life, a lot of hurt feelings, a lot of mistreatment, a lot of abuse, a lot of unfair, unjust, unkind things. But I thank God that I finally learned, in the midst of shaking them off, to also believe for my reward.

The expectation of God's reward gives you hope that God is not going to leave you defenseless, that He is going to do something for you. The next time people you know get angry about something, just say to them, "Shake it off." When you meet someone who is depressed, say, "Shake it off." If people you know are moping around because somebody has hurt their feelings, say, "Shake it off." I give you permission to preach this message to everyone who needs to hear it.

Trouble Will Come

You may think that you will be completely protected from encounters with trouble because you are serving God, but that is not true. As a matter of fact, if God sends you out to minister to others, you are almost sure to have trouble. But, like the three Hebrew children who were cast into the fiery furnace, you can expect to come through the fires of testing without even smelling like smoke just as Shadrach, Meshach, and Abednego did (see Daniel 3:23-27).

Jesus gave His disciples authority over the unclean spirits that would try to bring trouble to them. He also told His disciples what to do if the people they were trying to reach rejected them:

> And He called to Him the Twelve [apostles] and began to send them out [as His ambassadors] two by two and gave them authority *and* power over the unclean spirits.
>
> He charged them to take nothing for their journey except a walking stick—no bread, no wallet for a collection bag, no money in their belts (girdles, purses)—
>
> But to go with sandals on their feet and not to put on two tunics (undergarments).
>
> And He told them, Wherever you go into a house, stay there until you leave that place.
>
> And if any community will not receive *and* accept *and* welcome you, and they refuse to listen to you, when you depart, shake off the dust that is on your feet, for a testimony against them. *Truly I tell you, it will be more tolerable for Sodom and Gomorrah in the judgment day than for that town.* (Mark 6:7-10)

Jesus was showing all of us that He will provide everything needed to serve Him. The disciples did not need extra clothes or money. They were given authority over the trouble that would come against them, and if anyone rejected them, they were to simply "shake it off." So they went out and preached everywhere the message of repentance and salvation.

If you are going to be used by God, or if you are going to walk with God, you will experience a certain amount of rejection. And more than likely that rejection will come from the people who matter the most to you. It may come from family members or close friends.

If God touches you, and you want to go deeper with Him than some of your church friends, even they are likely to reject you. People just do not want others to go where they are not willing to go themselves. If they want to pursue carnal interests, and you want to walk in the Spirit, they may openly hate you for your choice.

Jesus said of the people of His day who resisted and opposed Him, "They hated Me without a cause" (John 15:25). It really struck me one day how sad that was. Jesus tried to be good to people, but instead of loving and appreciating Him for it, they hated Him.

Joseph had a dream, and his brothers hated him for it (see Genesis 37:5). Stephen was full of grace and power and worked great wonders and miracles among the people, but religious leaders hated him for his intelligence and wisdom and the inspiration of the Spirit by Whom he spoke, so they had him arrested and eventually stoned (see Acts 6:8-12; 7:58).

It is amazing how easy it is to draw hatred, jealousy, and envy from others. If you try to be good, somebody will hate you for it. But if you respond to them with the same anger they display toward you, you are keeping yourself from being blessed. Do not let people pull you down to their level—shake it off and step up.

It is hard to shake off rejection. It hurts. But it hurts even more to live by feelings. Learn to shake off the dust of rejection and disappointment.

One time I was trying to help someone, and I really felt that I was doing the right thing. I am always very busy, and I never have to look for something to do, so I felt that I was really making a sacrifice of time and effort by trying to help this person. But no matter what I did, this individual felt that it was never enough, and so I was getting upset about it.

I felt that God wanted me to help this person because it was my Christian duty. But it seemed that despite all my best efforts, nothing I did was successful or even understood or appreciated. I finally got a breakthrough when I realized that my responsibility was to *try* to help that person, but that I was not responsible for that individual's joy.

A lot of times, we want everybody to be happy with everything we are doing. But we have to get over thinking that everybody is going to be happy with everything we do. We have to do what we believe is right, what we believe God is leading us to do, but we have to realize that everybody is responsible for his or her own joy.

Jesus told His disciples to go preach. They did what they were supposed to do. But He told them that if people did not receive them or their message, they were not to let the indifference of others become a stumbling block to their own call.

Do not give up your ministry, or sit and cry pitifully for hours, just because everybody does not receive you, or appreciate you. Shake it off and press on to the next town, to the next person who needs to hear your testimony of what God has done in your life.

If rejection stops you cold in your tracks, then the spirit of rejection wins. You cannot stop doing what is right just because somebody does not like what you are doing.

As a matter of fact, I would venture to say that almost every time God is ready to promote you and bring you to the next level, you will experience an attack of rejection at the place where you are now. Satan will use rejection to try to keep you where you are or even to bring you down from there.

That is why so many people are rejected by their own family members when they get filled with the Holy Spirit. They go home all excited to tell everyone that they are living their lives for the Lord, only to discover that they are suddenly the "strange one" in the family. Satan uses the people who matter most to them to reject them and try to cause them to turn back to their old ways.

Step Up a Level

Like the donkey in the well, you need to shake off each shovel full of abuse and rejection and use it to keep stepping up a level until you are free to enjoy the life God has planned for you. You have already come into a new level with God. Your faith is already stronger today than it was yesterday. You are more prepared for the next time abuse is flung at you.

From this day forward, you will walk into a more powerful level with God because you have determined to be faithful to Him, no matter what. You are more dangerous to the enemy when you receive the power of the indwelling Holy Ghost.

Because you believe on Jesus and receive His Holy Spirit, you can pray and receive God's best in your life. You are free to press on toward the reward of God, and your testimony will do great damage to the devil's work. As a result, he is going to influence as many people as possible to become angry about it and to criticize and oppose you.

But remember the donkey: humble yourself and shake it off. Use what the enemy plans against you to move one step closer to the place God wants you to be.

For example, Dave and I were asked to leave our home church when God started moving in our life, but then God led us to another church where the pastor accepted us, and covered us with prayer and blessing.

The Bible says that we are not at war against flesh and blood, but against principalities and powers and wickedness in high places (see Ephesians 6:12). Satan will continue to try to use people to keep us from going forward. If possible, he will use people whom we know and love so that the wounds from their rejection and disapproval will be deep and painful.

Sometimes we fear the disapproval of people so much that we will not step up to the next level with God because we already know that somebody is not going to like it. It is amazing how many times we bow down to people when we should be bowing down to God.

Jesus said, "He who hears *and* heeds you [disciples] hears *and* heeds Me; and he who slights *and* rejects you slights *and* rejects Me; and he who slights *and* rejects Me slights *and* rejects Him who sent Me" (Luke 10:16). He was telling us not to take rejection personally. If people are rejecting us when we are following the Lord, then they are rejecting Jesus and the Father.

Now, understand that before you even gave your heart to the Lord, the devil recognized God's plan for you and did everything he could to keep you from receiving it. It is possible that the bigger the call on your life, the greater the abuse that comes against you. If you consider warfare in the spiritual world in the light of God's Word, you will understand that Satan sent all the trouble that has come upon you because he knew that God was pursuing you to bless you.

But Jehovah is the Lord of hosts—the Lord of the armies. He is fighting for you, and that makes you more than a conqueror. The battle over you has already been won, and you are promised a double blessing for your former trouble.

STAY FULL OF THE JOY OF THE LORD

The apostle Paul said, "Now am I trying to win the favor of men, or of God? Do I seek to please men? If I were still seeking popularity with men, I should not be a bond servant of Christ (the Messiah)" (Galatians 1:10).

We can see from this next passage of Scripture that Paul learned to shake off rejection and continue in joy:

> And so the Word of the Lord [concerning eternal salvation through Christ] scattered *and* spread throughout the whole region.
>
> But the Jews stirred up the devout women of high rank and the outstanding men of the town, and instigated perse-

> cution against Paul and Barnabas and drove them out of their boundaries.
>
> But [the apostles] shook off the dust from their feet against them and went to Iconium.
>
> And the disciples were continually filled [throughout their souls] with joy and the Holy Spirit. (Acts 13:49-52)

Stay continually filled with joy and the Holy Spirit throughout your soul; keep your mind, will, and emotions fixed on the joy that is available through the indwelling presence of the Lord. You will lose your joy if you get concerned about what everybody thinks about you. Shake off your self-consciousness and "be filled *and* stimulated with the [Holy] Spirit" (Ephesians 5:18). Remain full of joy no matter what trouble comes against you. Do your best to do what you believe God wants you to do in every situation.

If people do not have enough love to show you a little mercy just because you do not do everything the way they want you to, then that is between them and God. Do not live your life to be popular; live it to do God's will.

To obey God, Joseph had to shake off many hurts and disappointments such as the betrayal of his brothers, the lies of Potipher's wife, and the forgotten promise of the butler he had helped. But the result of pressing on was that Joseph was put in charge everywhere he went. God gave him a double recompense for his troubles, and he was greatly blessed (see Genesis 37-Exodus 1).

Likewise, people did not like Daniel because he was a godly man who kept shaking off rejection. He was so disliked that he was thrown into a den of hungry lions, but God shut the mouths of the lions. When the king saw what God had done for Daniel, he proclaimed: "I make a decree that in all my royal dominion men must tremble and fear before the God of Daniel, for He is the living God, enduring *and* steadfast forever, and His kingdom shall not be destroyed and His dominion shall be even to the end [of the world]" (Daniel 6:26).

Daniel's steadfast walk with God inspired an entire nation to believe that God "is a Savior and Deliverer, and He works signs and wonders in the heavens and on the earth—He Who has delivered Daniel from the power of the lions" (Daniel 6:27).

In Paul's letter to the Thessalonians, beginning in 2 Thessalonians 1:3, he gave thanks because believers were growing in faith, their love for each other was increasing, and they were steadfast in the midst of persecutions and crushing distresses.

In verse 6, Paul reassured believers that God would repay with distress and affliction those who distressed and afflicted them. Then he wrote of God's determination to reward them:

> And to [recompense] you who are so distressed *and* afflicted [by granting you] relief *and* rest along with us [your fellow sufferers] when the Lord Jesus is revealed from heaven with His mighty angels in a flame of fire,
>
> To deal out retribution (chastisement and vengeance) upon those who do not know *or* perceive *or* become acquainted with God, and [upon those] who ignore *and* refuse to obey the Gospel of our Lord Jesus *Christ*" (2 Thessalonians 1:7-8).

So if you are persecuted for doing what is right in the eyes of God, rejoice. The apostle Peter said, "[After all] what kind of glory [is there in it] if, when you do wrong and are punished for it, you take it patiently? But if you bear patiently with suffering [which results] when you do right *and* that is undeserved, it is acceptable *and* pleasing to God" (1 Peter 2:20).

When you suffer for doing right, Jesus calls you blessed, saying: "Blessed *and* happy *and* enviably fortunate *and* spiritually prosperous (in the state in which the born-again child of God enjoys and finds satisfaction in God's favor and salvation, regardless of his outward conditions) are those who are persecuted for righteousness' sake (for being and doing right), for theirs is the kingdom of heaven!" (Matthew 5:10)

Peter had to shake off failure, Paul had to shake off rejection, and you are going to have to shake off both failure and rejection if you want to be used by God. But a double reward is in store for you.

Shake off unforgiveness, resentment, trouble, and self-pity. Shake off rejection, offense, betrayal, gossip, judgment, and the kiss of Judas. Shake off arguments with relatives, close friends, and strangers. Shake off your own failures and mistakes. Shake off disappointment over your own imperfection.

Just get over it, and go on.

The season for mourning is over. It is time to rejoice.

28

Miraculous Reward

As I was proofreading the manuscript for the first release of this book, God moved in a mighty way and brought deliverance and healing to the relationship between my father and me. I do not believe it was accidental that a miraculous conclusion of my story came in time for me to incorporate it into this book.

Although I had forgiven my father, our relationship had remained strained and uncomfortable. He had never fully accepted responsibility for his acts or faced how devastating his behavior was to my life. Through the years, I tried the best I knew how to have some kind of relationship with my parents, but it was a continual challenge.

I tried on two occasions to confront these issues with my father and mother, but neither of these efforts was successful. Each confrontation brought a lot of anger, upset, and blame, without any real conclusion. At least the door had been opened, and God was working in secret, behind the scenes, even when it seemed that nothing would ever change.

After I had moved my parents to live near me, God began

dealing with me about the biblical command to "honor your father and mother" (see Exodus 20:12). I must be truthful and say that although I was willing to honor them and desired to do so, I was baffled as to how to go about it. I visited them, called them, prayed for them, and took them presents, but still the Lord would say to me, "Honor your father and mother." I knew He was trying to show me something, but I could not grasp what it was.

Finally, one evening as I heard again, "Honor your father and mother," I told the Lord that I had done everything for them I knew to do, and that I did not know what else it was He wanted.

Then I heard Him say, "Honor them in your heart," to which I replied, "For what can I honor them?" He showed me that I could honor them and appreciate them, in my heart, for giving me my life, for feeding and clothing me, and for sending me to school.

I had been doing things for them outwardly, but God looks on the heart. I found it difficult to have fond feelings of appreciation when all I remembered was pain, but after hearing the same thing for a year from the Lord, I knew that it was important, so I did what He said.

I prayed, "Thank You, God, for my parents and the fact that they gave me my physical life. They brought me into the world; they fed me, clothed me, and sent me to school, and I honor them for doing so." I really saw what God was saying, and that moment I truly did appreciate the part my parents had played in my life.

About a week later, an issue arose concerning our newly released national television program, *Life In The Word*. I received news that my family members had seen the program and were urging my parents to watch it. My father and mother asked me what channel they could see the program on, and I realized that I needed to tell them I would be making reference to the abuse in my childhood because God had called me to help people who have been abused and mistreated.

I could not imagine what it would do to them if they tuned in their television set and heard me saying, "I come from a background of child abuse." I did not want to hurt them. I felt awful, but what could I do? Knowing that people find it easy to relate to me because I share my background so openly, I went into much prayer, and then called for a family conference with my husband, Dave, and our children. We decided that even though letting my parents know that what I was doing could finish off what little relationship we had left, I had to follow God's will for my life.

We went to visit them, and I shared the truth, telling them that I was not doing it to hurt them, but that I had no choice if I was to help the people God had called me to help.

I saw the miracle-working power of God!

My father and mother sat there and listened calmly. No anger was displayed; there were no accusations, no running from the truth.

My father then shared with Dave and me how sorry he was for what he had done to me. He said that God knew he was sorry and that if there was any way he could take it back, he would. He told me how he had been controlled and could not have prevented himself from what he was doing. He said that he had encountered abuse as a child himself, and was acting out of what he had learned and had become accustomed to.

He further shared that recently he had watched several television programs on abuse and had begun to realize from them how devastating sexual abuse really is. He released me to share whatever I needed to and told me not to worry about anything. He said that he wanted to build a relationship with me and try to be my father and my friend. My mother, of course, was ecstatic with joy at the thought of being able to have real relationships with her daughter, grandchildren, and great-grandchildren.

From that day forth, we started to see some changes in my father. He would go to church for special services on Easter or Christmas, but he never really said too much about it. He still had not given his heart to Jesus, and he was still difficult to get along with. Eventually, my mother told me that she felt that God might be dealing with my father. She said, "I have found him several times, sitting on the edge of his bed crying."

Then, one Thanksgiving morning my mother called and said, "Your dad is too sick to go to the family dinner today. He wishes he could come, but he just feels too bad, but he wants to know if you and Dave will come over and see him. He wants to talk to you about something."

So we went over, and the minute we walked into the room he started crying. He said, "I just need to tell you how sorry I am for what I did to you. I have wanted to say something about it for three years, but I just did not have the guts."

Those were his exact words. It is interesting to look back and see that it had been *three years* since we bought my parents the house and moved them to live near us. So our initial act of obedience to the Lord's direction was a seed that had been planted to break the devil's back in my father's situation. Then he wept with true repentance. I said, "It's all right, Daddy, I forgive you."

He asked Dave to forgive him too, and Dave said, "I forgive you."

Then I said to my father, "Do you want to receive Christ as your Savior?"

And he said, "Yes."

Because he had truly repented, it was totally different this time when he prayed. He received the Lord, and though he struggled with doubt for several days, thinking that he had been too bad to be forgiven, he finally asked to be baptized.

We baptized my dad ten days later. I can tell you honestly that I have never seen such a change in a person's character. He is still sick, and he feels bad all the time, but he never really complains. He is actually one of the sweetest men I know.

Did my dad pay the price for what he did? Absolutely! He is old and does not have a lot of friends. He cannot really get around. But I truly believe that showing him love, consistent love, and obeying God by honoring him in my heart, is what finally tore down that wall around him and caused him to repent.

My husband, Dave, told my dad that the day of his repentance was one of the greatest days in his life. As for me, I now fully understand God's promise, spoken through the prophet Isaiah: "Instead of your [former] shame you shall have a twofold recompense; instead of dishonor *and* reproach [your people] shall rejoice in their portion. Therefore in their land they shall possess double [what they had forfeited]; everlasting joy shall be theirs" (Isaiah 61:7). We have received a double blessing! God has restored both the abused *and the abuser!*

God is faithful! Dream big dreams, and never stop hoping!

Notes

1. James Strong, "Greek Dictionary of the New Testament," *Strong's Exhaustive Concordance of the Bible* (Nashville: Abingdon, 1890), p. 39, entry #2588, s.v. "heart(ed)," Luke 4:18.
2. Strong, p. 69, entry #4937, s.v. "broken," Luke 4:18.
3. *Merriam-Webster's Collegiate Dictionary, Tenth Edition*, s.v. "abuse."
4. To hear my complete testimony, write and ask for my tape album titled "Trophies of God's Grace."
5. I also have available a series of tapes called "Loving God, Loving Yourself, and Loving Others" that you can order from our ministry address.
6. To learn more about deliverance from guilt and condemnation, write me and ask for my four-tape series on this subject, *Guilt and Condemnation.*
7. Strong,"Hebrew and Chaldee Dictionary," p. 19, entry #954, s.v. "ashamed," Genesis 2:25.
8. *Webster's New World Dictionary*, 3d college ed., s.v. "confound."
9. Ibid., s.v. "damn."
10. If you would like more teaching on God's grace, write and ask for my six-tape album titled "Grace, Grace, and More Grace."

11. *Merriam-Webster's Collegiate Dictionary, Tenth Edition*, s.v. "covet."
12. Ibid., s.v. "envy."
13. Ibid., s.v. "jealousy."
14. Ibid., s.v. "drink."
15. (Eugene, OR: Harvest House, 1986), p. 13.

Bibliography

Backus, William, Ph.D. *Telling Each Other the Truth—The Art of True Communication*. Bethany House Publishers, Minneapolis, Minnesota, 1985.

Backus, William and Chapian, Marie. *Telling Yourself the Truth*. Bethany House Publishers, Minneapolis, Minnesota, 1980.

Beattie, Melody. *Co-dependent No More—How To Stop Controlling Others and Start Caring for Yourself*. Harper & Row, Publishers, Inc., New York, New York, by arrangement with the Hazelden Foundation, 1987.

Carlson, David E. *Counseling and Self-Esteem*. Word, Inc., Waco, Texas, 1988.

Carter, Les. *Putting the Past Behind—Biblical Solutions to Your Unmet Needs*. Moody Press, Chicago, Illinois, 1989.

Galloway, Dale E. *Confidence Without Conceit*. Fleming H. Revell Company, Old Tappan, New Jersey, 1989.

Grant, Dave E. *The Great Lover's Manifesto*. Harvest House Publishers, Eugene, Oregon, 1986.

Hart, Dr. Archibald D. *Healing Life's Hidden Addictions—Overcoming the Closet Compulsions That Waste Your Time and Control Your Life*. Vine Books, a division of Servant Publications, Ann Arbor, Michigan, 1990.

Holley, Debbie. "The Trickle-Down Theory of Conditional Love," "The Trickle-Down Theory of Unconditional Love." St. Louis, Missouri.

LaHaye, Tim. *Spirit-Controlled Temperament.* Post Inc., © LaMesa, California, for Tyndale House Publishers, Inc., Wheaton, Illinois, 1966.

Littauer, Florence. *Discovering the Real You by Uncovering the Roots of Your Personality Tree.* Word Books, Waco, Texas, 1986.

McGinnis, Alan Loy. *Confidence—How To Succeed at Being Yourself.* Augsburg Publishing House, Minneapolis, Minnesota, 1987.

Saunders, Molly. *Bulimia! Help Me, Lord!* Destiny Image Publishers, Shippensburg, Pennsylvania, 1988.

Solomon, Charles R., Ed.D. *The Ins and Outs of Rejection.* Heritage House Publications, Littleton, Colorado, 1976.

Sumrall, Lester. *Overcoming Compulsive Desires—How To Find Lasting Freedom.* Creation House, Lake Mary, Florida, 1990.

Walters, Richard P., Ph.D. *Counseling for Problems of Self-Control.* Word, Inc., Waco, Texas, 1987.

About the Author

Joyce Meyer has been teaching the Word of God since 1976 and in full-time ministry since 1980. She is the bestselling author of more than sixty inspirational books, including *In Pursuit of Peace, How to Hear from God*, *Knowing God Intimately*, and *Battlefield of the Mind*. She has also released thousands of teaching cassettes and a complete video library. Joyce's *Enjoying Everyday Life* radio and television programs are broadcast around the world, and she travels extensively conducting conferences. Joyce and her husband, Dave, are the parents of four grown children and make their home in St. Louis, Missouri.

To contact the author write:

Joyce Meyer Ministries
P.O. Box 655
Fenton, Missouri 63026
or call: (636) 349-0303
Internet Address: www.joycemeyer.org

Please include your testimony or help received from this book when you write. Your prayer requests are welcome.

To contact the author

In Canada, please write:

Joyce Meyer Ministries Canada, Inc.
Lambeth Box 1300
London, ON N6P 1T5
or call: (636) 349-0303

In Australia, please write:

Joyce Meyer Ministries-Australia
Locked Bag 77
Mansfield Delivery Centre
Queensland 4122
or call: 07 3349 1200

In England, please write:

Joyce Meyer Ministries
P.O. Box 1549
Windsor
SL4 1GT
or call: (0) 1753-831102

JOYCE MEYER TITLES

Battlefield of the Mind
Battlefield of the Mind Study Guide
Approval Addiction
Ending Your Day Right
In Pursuit of Peace
The Secret Power of Speaking God's Word
Seven Things That Steal Your Joy
Starting Your Day Right
Beauty for Ashes Revised Edition
How to Hear from God
How to Hear from God Study Guide
Knowing God Intimately
The Power of Forgiveness
The Power of Determination
The Power of Being Positive
The Secrets of Spiritual Power
The Battle Belongs to the Lord
Secrets to Exceptional Living
Eight Ways to Keep the Devil Under Your Feet
Teenagers Are People Too!
Filled with the Spirit
Celebration of Simplicity
The Joy of Believing Prayer
Never Lose Heart
Being the Person God Made You to Be
A Leader in the Making
"Good Morning, This Is God!" Gift Book
Jesus—Name Above All Names
"Good Morning, This Is God!" Daily Calendar

Making Marriage Work (Previously published as *Help Me—I'm Married!*)
Reduce Me to Love
Be Healed in Jesus' Name
How to Succeed at Being Yourself
Eat and Stay Thin
Weary Warriors, Fainting Saints
Life in the Word Journal
Life in the Word Devotional
Be Anxious for Nothing
Be Anxious for Nothing Study Guide
Straight Talk Omnibus
Straight Talk on Loneliness
Straight Talk on Fear
Straight Talk on Insecurity
Straight Talk on Discouragement
Straight Talk on Worry
Straight Talk on Depression
Straight Talk on Stress
Don't Dread
Managing Your Emotions
Healing the Brokenhearted
Me and My Big Mouth!
Me and My Big Mouth! Study Guide
Prepare to Prosper
Do It Afraid!
Expect a Move of God in Your Life... Suddenly!
Enjoying Where You Are on the Way to Where You Are Going
The Most Important Decision You Will Ever Make
When, God, When?
Why, God, Why?
The Word, the Name, the Blood

Tell Them I Love Them
Peace
The Root of Rejection
If Not for the Grace of God
If Not for the Grace of God Study Guide

JOYCE MEYER SPANISH TITLES

Las Siete Cosas Que Te Roban el Gozo
(Seven Things That Steal Your Joy)
Empezando Tu Día Bien (Starting Your Day Right)

BY DAVE MEYER

Life Lines

CPSIA information can be obtained
at www.ICGtesting.com
Printed in the USA
LVHW010816060620
657559LV00029B/974

9 780446 691154